ACTING Natural

Monologs, Dialogs and Playlets For Teens

PEG
KEHRET

MERIWETHER PUBLISHING LTD.
Colorado Springs, Colorado

Meriwether Publishing Ltd., Publisher
P.O. Box 7710
Colorado Springs, CO 80933

Editor: Arthur L. Zapel
Typesetting: Susan Trinko
Cover design: Tom Myers
Cover painting: Arthur L. Zapel

Library of Congress Cataloging-in-Publication Data

Kehret, Peg.
    Acting natural : monologs, dialogs, and playlets for teens / by Peg Kehret.
        p.   cm.
    ISBN 0-916260-84-4
    1. Acting   2. Monologues   3. Dialogues   4. Young adult drama,
    American.   5. Teenagers--Drama.   I. Title.
    PN2080.K33   1991
  812'.54--dc20   91-43552
                                           CIP

4   5   6   7   8   9   02   01   00   99   98

For Chelsea Elizabeth
November 24, 1990

AUTHOR'S NOTE:

I have assigned names and genders to most of the roles in this book. However, many parts can be played by either a female or a male, and names can be changed, as desired.

TABLE OF CONTENTS

Monologs

M = Male   F = Female   O = Optional

Dialogs

M = Male   F = Female   O = Optional

Playlets

First number in ( ) denotes total cast; second and third numbers specify gender.   M = Male   F = Female   Opt. = Optional

PREFACE

It is rare for dramatic material to portray teens with respect, to address the issues they are interested in, and to stimulate their thinking in new directions. In *Acting Natural*, I attempt to do all of this and more.

Young people today are faced with the enormous challenge of forming their opinions on a wide variety of topics. Often they need help in seeing all sides of complex issues. I expect this book to stimulate thinking and provoke discussion. It is not enough to entertain; my purpose here is also to stretch minds and hearts by introducing fresh ideas and exploring various points of view, in language that young actors find comfortable and natural. I want to help them remove the blinders of unawareness, apathy and self-absorption.

I also hope to free the young actors who read these lines from any reluctance to voice their opinions and feelings. Teens are often reticent to state their views, fearing that others will disagree. Because it is easier to speak as a character, rather than as oneself, drama is a tool which encourages communication. The monologs, dialogs and playlets in *Acting Natural* allow teens to express their feelings through a character, enabling actors and audience to confidently assess ideas, to discuss all sides of controversial topics, and to share their conclusions.

These 60 pieces discuss teen pregnancy, family relationships, preoccupation with weight, ecology, exclusive dating, animal rights, materialism, outgrowing a friendship, and dozens of other subjects of high interest to teens. I have tried to approach each topic with grace, humor, and an open mind, using realistic situations and authentic dialogue.

It is my hope that those who use this book will laugh and think, and encourage each other to respond honestly. Most of all, I hope they will find useful insights into the problems and joys of growing up.

Peg Kehret

FOREWORD

I became acquainted with Peg Kehret back in 1975. It was then that *The Spirit of Happy Hollow* (later shortened to *Spirit*) won our very first nationwide playwriting award here at Northern Michigan University. Her "thoughtful comedy" had wit, charm, poignancy and relevance—characteristics, I was soon to discover, of the playwright herself. She also surprised and thrilled me by changing the leading character's name to Clara Panowski when the play was published. Her thoughtful gesture has never been forgotten.

After devouring *Acting Natural*, I am delighted to report that those qualities that initially drew me to her work have been honed and fine tuned. Her observations of young adults and the world in which they live are as acute, as perceptive and as fresh as tomorrow's headlines.

Kehret does not shy away from such sometimes unsettling topics as teenage sex (*Prom Night Party*), unwed mothers (*A Baby of My Own*), homosexuality (*Sticks and Stones*), drinking and driving (*One Every Twenty-Two Minutes* and *Only A Few Beers*) and divorce (*Happy Endings*). She confronts these very real teen problems with insight, good taste and compassion.

Acting Natural also zeros in upon wider issues that affect adults as well as teens. *Going for Broke* deals with the inequities of rich vs. poor; *Human Beans* reminds us that frogs are "human," too, and that we must follow through with the courage of our convictions; *Will I Kill You, If I Have To?* is a chilling look inside the minds of two young soldiers as they come to grips with the terrible realities of war and death; *Heartbeats* shows teens' efforts to save the animal and wildlife victims of an oil slick; *The Simple Life* reminds us how important the earth's resources are; *Transformation* ponders what life would be like if *we* were animals; and *Five Minutes to Change the World* offers some practical suggestions on how to do just that.

Don't be misled; Peg Kehret is a pixie at heart with a wry and wonderful sense of humor. Just take a look at *Yum, Yum, Broccoli; Baseball Fanatic; Sisterly Love; Letter from Camp* (shades of Allan Sherman); and *Dear Jan Slander*, a hysterical spoof of advice to the lovelorn.

I must confess that several of my favorites are those that "sneak up" on you and leave you with a smile on your face as well as a lump in your throat. Such is the case with *I'll Be There, Friends Forever, Flowers Won't Bring Billy Back* and *Red Roses for A Dead Cat*. But I suspect my real favorite is *My Head Is Full of Starshine*. This monolog may well be a mini-autobiography of Peg Kehret herself—of any writer, any real artist.

Having taught high school for a number of years, I am well aware of just how difficult it is to find quality material that speaks to young adults, is within the grasp of their developing thespian talents, and that runs the gamut of topics and genre. Such is the welcome case with this wonderful collection of monologs, dialogs and playlets.

Acting Natural can certainly be used in the speech and drama classroom, for competitions, and as discussion starters. I would also highly recommend this book for psychology and sociology classes, as well as for health and family living courses.

When all is said and done, may I suggest that you simply pick up *Acting Natural* and read it from cover to cover for pure pleasure. You'll find, as I have, that it's as good a read as any book on the best-seller list! Enjoy!

James A. Panowski, Ph.D.
Director, Forest Roberts Theatre
Northern Michigan University

Monologs

UNNECESSARY RULES

1   Mrs. Morgan has a rule about not chewing gum in class.
2 Did you ever hear anything so ridiculous? What does chewing
3 gum have to do with learning mathematics? I can do fractions
4 just as well with gum in my mouth as I can without it. It bugs
5 me when people have rules for no reason.
6   Mrs. Morgan is big on rules. For her math class, we have
7 to turn in our weekly homework no later than noon on Friday.
8 Why noon? What is so sacred about twelve o'clock? I'm not
9 Cinderella.
10   Once I forgot to turn in my homework during class, so I
11 took it to her Friday afternoon, after school. Do you know what
12 she did? She gave me an extra assignment, due on Monday
13 morning. Talk about unfair. Why should I have to do homework
14 on the weekend?
15   Supposedly, I take Mrs. Morgan's class in order to learn
16 math, but sometimes it seems I'm learning more about how to
17 follow unnecessary rules than I am about numbers. My mother
18 says there are reasons for school rules. Sure there are. Person-
19 ally, I think the reason is because Mrs. Morgan wants to have
20 power over the students.
21   Last week, I decided to test her. I broke one of her rules
22 on purpose, to see what would happen. We had a one-page
23 home test, where we got to take the test home and use as much
24 time as we wanted to answer the questions. Theoretically,
25 everyone should get one hundred percent of the answers right
26 on a home test, since we are allowed to use the textbooks.
27   I worked hard on my home test, and I was positive I got
28 everything right. But Mrs. Morgan had another of her ridicu-
29 lous rules this time. "The home test must be mounted on con-
30 struction paper or cardboard." Did you ever hear of anything
31 so dumb? Why should we have to mount our math tests on
32 heavy paper? So I didn't. I wanted to see if I would get an A
33 for my correct answers or if she would downgrade me because

1   of her silly rule.
2   Here is what happened: I got the A. However, I had to
3   stay after school that afternoon and scrape gum off the bottoms
4   of the chairs. Talk about gross! Big wads of purple gum and
5   gray gum, stuck right on the furniture. I pried them off with a
6   paint scraper. It was disgusting.
7   While I was doing that, Mrs. Morgan hung all the home
8   tests in the gymnasium, because there was an Open House for
9   parents the next night. That is, she hung all the tests except
10 mine. Since mine was not mounted on heavy paper, it didn't
11 work for the display.
12   My parents and I went to the Open House. I waited for
13 them to notice that my math test wasn't there with the others.
14 I thought they would be upset and would tell Mrs. Morgan what
15 they thought of her stupid rules. Instead, do you know what
16 my parents said? They said Mrs. Morgan is preparing us for
17 the real world. They said when I grow up, I will have to follow
18 certain rules that my employer has and I might just as well
19 learn to do it gracefully.
20   I said what possible difference does it make if I turn in
21 my homework at noon on Friday or at three-thirty? So my dad
22 asked Mrs. Morgan about that. She said she has a free period
23 from one until two on Fridays, so she can correct the homework
24 papers then. Otherwise, she has to take them home with her
25 and do them on the weekend. She tries to keep weekends for
26 her family.
27   Then she said something else that completely astounded
28 me. She said she was sorry she had neglected to make her
29 reasons clear to me. She said in the future, she would try to be
30 sure I understood why she had certain rules. She even said it's
31 good that I question rules and think for myself instead of blindly
32 doing everything I'm told.
33   Can you believe it? Mrs. Morgan stood up for me! Maybe
34 she isn't power hungry, after all.
35

YUM, YUM, BROCCOLI

1   I have a secret. Nobody knows it—not my parents or my
2 brother. Not even my best friend. I've heard it isn't good to
3 keep a secret all bottled up inside yourself. If you do, some day
4 the bottle will explode and you'll end up with shattered nerves,
5 so I've decided to confess my secret to you.
6   Here it is. I do not have a food problem. Repeat: I do *not*
7 have any problems with food.
8   Shocking, isn't it? Everyone else in the universe has what's
9 called an eating disorder. Some of my friends are bulimic. Some
10 are allergic to wheat or milk or tomatoes. Some are anorexic.
11 Some are picky eaters who have never tasted anything green.
12 Some claim food addictions that produce overwhelming crav-
13 ings for marshmallows or French fries or salted cashews. At
14 noon in the school cafeteria, people play a conversational game
15 called, "My Food Addiction Is Worse than Your Food Addic-
16 tion."
17   When they finish with that, they talk about how dreadful
18 the school lunches are. I never say anything. How can I? I like
19 tuna sandwiches and macaroni casseroles and carrot sticks. I
20 like all the food that the other kids complain about. I even like
21 cauliflower. It's embarrassing.
22   Some people get up at night and sneak into the bathroom
23 to eat chocolate bars. I could never do that. Oh, I can under-
24 stand waking up and feeling hungry, although usually I roll
25 over and go back to sleep. Once in a great while, I'm hungry
26 enough to actually crawl out of my warm bed and put my bare
27 feet on the icy floor and walk to the kitchen for a slice of cold
28 pizza or some leftover apple pie. But I cannot imagine choosing
29 to eat it in the bathroom. Why not just sit at the table? Or curl
30 up on the sofa, wrapped snug in an afghan? Or even scurry
31 back to bed and prop up the pillow and eat there? Somehow,
32 the bathroom is not my idea of the proper atmosphere for eat-
33 ing. But judging from the number of people who tell me that

1   they sneak treats there, someone should open a restaurant
2   decorated with bathtubs and sinks. If they used toilets instead
3   of chairs, they'd probably make a fortune.
4   At least half the kids I know are on a diet. Make that
5   two-thirds. My friends aren't fat. They're just scared that they
6   might get fat someday if they don't go on a diet now. They say
7   things like, "I love chocolate shakes, but I'll just have a diet
8   soda." That is one of the saddest sentences I've ever heard. If
9   you really love chocolate shakes, why not have one now and
10   then and cut back on calories somewhere else? I've decided
11   the people who say "I love chocolate shakes, but I'll just have
12   a diet soda" don't really want the chocolate shake. What they
13   want is to feel noble. I'm never sure if it spoils their fun or
14   increases it when I drink my chocolate shake in front of them.
15   Maybe I'd be more like everyone else if I quit eating break-
16   fast. I like breakfast. I always have orange juice or a grapefruit.
17   Cereal or toast. Milk. Sometimes even an egg. I do not know
18   one other person who eats a traditional breakfast. They drink
19   prepared diet drinks or they eat chocolate donuts, or both.
20   Most common of all, they skip breakfast entirely.
21   It worries me that I'm so different. I'm always hungry at
22   meal time, but I rarely snack in between. When I read those
23   weight charts that magazines sometimes print, I'm exactly the
24   perfect weight for my age and height. I like dessert, including
25   chocolate, but I can open a package of cookies and eat only
26   one. Clearly, there's something wrong with me.
27   Well, now you know my secret. I am the only person alive
28   who does not suffer from a food addiction and who is not on
29   a diet. No matter how hard I try to overcome it, I remain well
30   nourished and happy. Please don't tell anyone. I don't want
31   any pity.
32
33
34
35

EVERYTHING BAD
HAPPENS TO ME

1 Everything bad happens to me. I am jinxed. There must
2 be a witch doctor somewhere who has a voodoo doll of me for
3 people to stick pins into. Long, sharp pins. Why else would
4 everything go wrong in my life, when I have done absolutely
5 nothing to deserve such rotten luck?
6 For example: Last week, I was lying on the floor finishing
7 my semester workbook for biology and watching the ball game
8 on TV when I noticed that my dog, Comet, had an odd look on
9 his face. He looked as if he might have something in his mouth
10 that didn't taste good. Being a person who is kind to animals,
11 I was immediately concerned. First I said, "Drop it," several
12 times, hoping Comet would spit out whatever it was, but he
13 just sat there with enormous, sad eyes and his mouth shut.
14 Wondering if he might have a sore tooth, I tried to pry
15 open his jaws and look. This made Comet act even more un-
16 happy than before. He clenched his teeth tightly together and
17 whimpered softly.
18 Finally I let go of his head and sat back to watch the ball
19 game. It was third down and goal to go when Comet began to
20 gag. Probably every dog owner recognizes the sound of a pet
21 who is about to throw up. It creates instant panic as the owner
22 frantically looks for a newspaper to stick in front of the dog.
23 Pet owners know from experience that it is far easier to throw
24 out a newspaper than it is to clean the carpet.
25 Unfortunately, my instinct to grab a piece of paper was
26 faster than my reasoning ability. Comet gagged, I grabbed, and
27 before I realized what I was doing, he had urped all over my
28 biology workbook.
29 I slaved for six weeks on that workbook; there wasn't time
30 to do it over. I had to face my biology teacher the next morning
31 with a semester workbook that not only had big blotches on
32 most of the pages, but also had a distinctly unappealing odor.
33 When I complained to my mother that everything bad

1   happens to me, she hinted that if I had not been so engrossed
2   in the football game I was watching, I would have noticed what
3   I was sticking under Comet's heaving mouth.

4   I might have known I wouldn't get any sympathy from
5   her. She has been telling me for years that I should not watch
6   TV while I do my homework.

7   I had barely recovered from the Comet episode when the
8   great tree-planting disaster occurred. There's a new housing
9   development going in not far from where I live. It's sad to see
10   the trees being cut down and the land leveled. Late one after-
11   noon, as I watched the bulldozers finish their work, I spotted
12   a young tree growing right in their path. The next day, I knew
13   it would be gone.

14   As soon as the workers left, I got a shovel and went back
15   to the site. I dug up the sapling, which was about three feet
16   high, and dragged it home. I felt so good about saving the little
17   tree's life that I decided to plant it right outside my bedroom
18   window, where I could see it first thing every morning and last
19   thing every night. So many bad things happen to me; this would
20   be constant evidence of something good.

21   I had a hard time getting the hole big enough. For such a
22   short tree, there were an awful lot of roots. First I dug up a
23   round circle of grass. Then I kept going deeper. Several times,
24   my shovel clicked on a rock and I had to wiggle the shovel
25   back and forth to get through. I nearly had the hole deep enough
26   when my shovel went, *clunk*. From the sound of it, this rock
27   was huge. Wiggling the shovel didn't help. I had to push as
28   hard as I could, standing on the shovel with both feet, before
29   the shovel finally went deeper.

30   At last I got the tree in the hole, filled in the dirt, and
31   watered it. I went inside, sweaty, dirty and pleased with myself.
32   My father was home, and he was anything but pleased. He was
33   on the telephone with the cable TV company, complaining be-
34   cause the cable went out right in the middle of his favorite
35   program.

1   When he hung up, he said the company already had trucks
2 out trying to locate and correct the problem. He grumbled that
3 some idiot had cut the cable in half. Actually, he did not use
4 the word *idiot*, but there are certain things my father says which
5 I am not allowed to repeat.
6   I cannot repeat what he said a short time later, either,
7 when the cable TV people knocked on our door.
8   That last rock I hit with my shovel was not a rock at all.
9 It was the television cable. Our entire neighborhood was with-
10 out cable for three hours, and they all knew where the problem
11 was because the truck was parked right in front of my house.
12   As I said, bad things happen to me. I'm reminded of that
13 every morning and every night, when I look out my window
14 and see the tree, growing where Dad planted it, about six feet
15 from the original hole.
16
17
18
19
20
21
22
23
24
25
26
27
28
29
30
31
32
33
34
35

PAINTING THE ROCK

1   There's a big rock on the edge of town. It's visible from
2 the freeway. Every few weeks, someone paints a message on
3 the rock—something like "Nick Loves Julie." Or a group from
4 the senior class will paint their class year, futilely hoping it
5 will stay there forever, instead of getting painted over by the
6 juniors with *their* class year.

7   Ever since I first knew about the rock, I've had a burning
8 ambition to paint it. I would never paint my name and then
9 broadcast to the world my love for some girl. I don't even have
10 a date for next Saturday's dance, much less a love relationship
11 to announce. Besides, my parents would have a fit if they saw
12 my name there. They would say I had defaced public property,
13 although the rock has already been painted so many times I
14 don't think one more coat is going to make any difference. Still,
15 my parents would not be overjoyed if they learned I had
16 climbed the hill beside the freeway, paint brush in hand.

17   That's why I decided to do it after dark. Just in case any
18 of my parents' friends happened to be driving that section of
19 the freeway. I wore my black jeans and a dark jacket. I wore
20 a ski mask, too. Partly, the ski mask was so I couldn't be recog-
21 nized and partly it was because the air next to the freeway
22 smells like exhaust fumes, and I didn't want to pass out in the
23 middle of my paint job.

24   Usually, painting the rock is a group effort. I intended to
25 be the first person ever to pull off the job alone.

26   There would be one other big difference in my rock paint-
27 ing adventure. Everyone would like my message.

28   Often, the messages on the rock made people angry. When
29 the seniors painted their class year on the rock, the juniors got
30 mad. When the Republicans painted their candidate's name,
31 the Democrats had a fit. Sometimes, even things like "Nick
32 Loves Julie" create a ruckus, because it turns out that it wasn't
33 Nick who painted the rock at all, but Nick's buddies, who knew

1   Nick couldn't stand the sight of Julie, and who did it for a
2   practical joke. Julie wasn't too happy, either.
3   I elected to paint a message that would upset no one:
4   "Smile." That's all; just one, little, happy word—smile. Simple,
5   but perfect. I bought bright yellow paint, and laid my plans
6   carefully. I chose the night my parents go to their weekly bridge
7   club. I asked if I could use the other car for an hour or so. I
8   said I needed to go to the library. Notice, I did not say I planned
9   to use the car to go to the library. I was careful not to tell a lie.
10   As soon as Mom and Dad left that night, I put on my black
11   jeans, jacket, and ski mask. From the basement, I got the paint,
12   a brush, and an old rag, in case I made a mistake and had to
13   wipe off the rock.
14   I drove carefully. The last thing I wanted was to be noticed.
15   I planned to take the side road that parallels the freeway. I
16   would park there, climb over the fence, and scale the hill to
17   the rock.
18   My heart knocked against my ribs like it wanted to escape.
19   Sweat trickled down inside my black jacket. I took a couple of
20   deep breaths, trying to calm myself. It was stifling inside that
21   ski mask, but I didn't want to take it off when I was almost
22   there. I decided to get a cold drink. If I used a straw, I could
23   drink it through the mouth hole in the mask.
24   I pulled into the 7-11 parking lot, looked around to be sure
25   I didn't see anyone I knew, and hopped out of the car. As I
26   pushed open the door, a woman who was standing at the
27   magazine rack, gasped. I figured she was reading some juicy
28   gossip in *The National Enquirer*. I went past her toward the
29   counter. The clerk, instead of asking what I wanted, backed
30   away from me until she was flat against the wall.
31   I started to say, "Give me a large Coke, please," but I only
32   got as far as "Give me" when two burly guys who were buying
33   beer jumped me and pinned me to the floor.
34   One of them yelled, "Call the police!"
35   The clerk said, "I did. We have a silent alarm."

1   At that moment, three police officers rushed in.
2   "We got him," said the big ape who by then was sitting on
3   my stomach.
4   I won't give you a play-by-play account of what happened
5   next. It's too painful to remember. The synopsis is that the cops
6   frisked me, questioned me, searched my car, took me to the
7   station, and ultimately called my parents.
8   I had worried about what they would say if they found
9   out I painted "Smile" on the rock. It was nothing compared to
10   what they said when the cops called their bridge club and told
11   them I had been picked up for allegedly trying to rob a 7-11. It
12   didn't help when they insisted their son was at the library.
13   Reluctantly, I admitted my intent; the can of paint and the
14   brush offered proof. No charge was filed and, eventually, I was
15   allowed to leave.
16   I never did paint "Smile" on the rock. I didn't feel much
17   like smiling anyway.
18
19
20
21
22
23
24
25
26
27
28
29
30
31
32
33
34
35

LET'S HEAR IT
FOR THE ONE-PARENT FAMILY

1   It seems fashionable to blame society's ills on one-parent
2   families. Numerous studies make a point of stating the high
3   percentage of kids in trouble who live in one-parent homes.
4   The implication is that two parents always raise responsible,
5   law-abiding children, while one person raising kids alone is
6   destined to produce nothing but juvenile delinquents.

7   I want to set the record straight. One person can do just
8   as good a job of raising children as two people can. Even better.
9   For one thing, it's more fair. A kid in a two-parent home is
10   always outnumbered. I know. I live with both my parents, and
11   it is always two of them and one of me. Family conferences are
12   a joke.

13   It is discouraging to always be the minority vote. For
14   example, my parents are dieting and they're both fond of fish.
15   So what do we eat for dinner every night? You can bet it isn't
16   macaroni and cheese, or pizza, or any of the other foods I vote
17   for. No. We have tuna salad with no mayo, or poached halibut.

18   I said, "Let's have French fries on the side, just for the
19   halibut." Nobody laughed. When you're dieting, you lose more
20   than pounds; you lose your sense of humor.

21   My only hope of balancing the vote is if my parents have
22   another baby, a decision over which I have absolutely no control.

23   Then there's the matter of privacy. A kid who lives with
24   just one parent has some hope of occasionally spending time
25   unsupervised. Not me. You'd think my parents were parole
26   officers and I was a third-time offender, the way they keep
27   track of my whereabouts. Not that I have anything to hide, but
28   once in awhile it would be nice to be able to sit and stare into
29   space without having my mother suggest that I go outside and
30   shoot baskets.

31   She thinks I don't get enough fresh air. According to her,
32   ample fresh air prevents acne, boredom, and assorted upper
33   respiratory infections. My dad agrees, naturally.

1   I said if the air in our house is so polluted it causes acne,
2   then maybe I should move in with my friend, Chris, who is
3   allowed to watch all of the TV shows that I am not allowed to
4   watch. Chris, by the way, lives with only his father and he has
5   never been in trouble. Mom said if I wanted to see Chris, I could
6   invite him over to shoot baskets with me, which I did. We had
7   a blast playing Horse.
8   Theoretically, when two parents are on the scene, there
9   are more opportunities for cultural enrichment than if only one
10 parent is present. Maybe. My folks do take me to concerts, and
11 I know what the inside of an art gallery looks like. But Chris
12 and his dad go hiking, and they have a book about rocks, and
13 they try to identify all the different kinds that they find. Chris
14 has never been to the Opera House like I have, but he's been
15 to the band concerts in the park on Sunday afternoons. And
16 he does know a lot about agate and quartz and something called
17 Fool's Gold. He even has a fossil collection.
18   Would I change places with Chris? Do I really want to live
19 in a one-parent home?
20   Which parent?
21   No. Despite the diet dinners and the fresh air nagging and
22 the minority vote at family conferences, I can't imagine living
23 with only one of my parents.
24   The odd thing is: Chris says he can't imagine having some-
25 one besides his dad around all the time.
26   As I said, the surveys are wrong. It isn't important how
27 many parents you live with. What matters is whether they love
28 you.
29
30
31
32
33
34
35

HAPPY ENDINGS

1   Once upon a time there was a little kid—me—who believed
2   in fairy stories. I believed there really was a Peter Rabbit. I
3   believed that somewhere in a far-away castle, Sleeping Beauty
4   and her Prince were living happily ever after. I even believed
5   that seven dwarfs still marched off to work in the mines every
6   morning, cheerfully whistling.
7   Life was simpler back in my once-upon-a-time years. When
8   I looked at the pictures in my books, I had faith that the whole
9   world would somehow have a happy ending.
10   I was ten when I learned that real life is different from
11   fiction. That's how old I was when my mom and dad got a
12   divorce. They were civil about it, and they both tried to spend
13   time with me and my sister. They told us the divorce didn't
14   have anything to do with how they feel about us. As Mom put
15   it, they tried to "minimize the impact on the children."
16   The trouble is, even with minimizing the impact, that di-
17   vorce felt like a wheelbarrow load of cement on my shoulders.
18   I understood why they did it, but I wished they hadn't. I wished
19   they could have lived happily ever after.
20   The accident happened when I was twelve. A station
21   wagon sideswiped my sister's bike. She has a limp now—she
22   will always have a limp—and I realized that sometimes bad
23   things happen through no fault of our own. Innocent people
24   are victims.
25   There was a whole series of misfortunes that year. Besides
26   Shannon's accident, my Grandma broke her hip, and our cat,
27   Rhino, died, and my best friend, Jackie, moved to North Dakota.
28   It was a rotten year.
29   One day, when I was feeling really down, I started to clean
30   out my closet. I found all of my old picture books, and I spent
31   a couple of hours reading them again.
32   At first, as I paged through the familiar stories, I felt cyn-
33   ical, thinking I had been purposely misled as a child. But the

1 more I read, the more I relaxed. I cheered once again as Jack
2 raced down the beanstalk and escaped from the giant. I laughed
3 at the foolish wolf in Grannie's clothing, confident that he would
4 soon get his comeuppance from the wood chopper. The familiar
5 pictures comforted me.
6   My spirits soared because Peter Rabbit and Snow White
7 and Red Riding Hood were alive and well in my imagination.
8 No matter what disasters happen in reality, my pretend friends
9 will never change.
10   Re-reading my childhood books taught me something else.
11 Although real life is sometimes sad, in my mind I can create
12 whatever kind of world I choose. I can remember how silky
13 Rhino's fur felt when I petted him, and how he rumbled when
14 he purred. I can write to Jackie. Now that Shannon doesn't
15 take ballet lessons anymore, we have time to work on the doll
16 house that we're building together. Through the power of imag-
17 ination and love, I can overcome the sad events and turn them
18 into joys.
19   Perhaps that's why I love my books. They have taught me
20 to appreciate the good things that happen and to do what I can
21 to make every ending a happy one. "Once upon a time" is still
22 the doorway to a magical world and, in some ways, I will always
23 be a little kid who believes in fairy stories.
24
25
26
27
28
29
30
31
32
33
34
35

UNPAID BABY SITTER

1   I have to baby-sit my little brothers again tonight. It isn't
2 fair! Just because I'm the oldest, why do I have to take care of
3 them all the time? I suggested that I ought to at least get paid
4 for baby-sitting, but my dad said every family member is ex-
5 pected to contribute what they can, and the best thing I can
6 contribute right now is to take care of my brothers.
7   My little brothers sure as heck don't contribute anything.
8 P.J. makes messes wherever he goes, and Michael whines all
9 the time. This would have been a great family if I had been an
10 only child, but my parents failed to see that until it was too late.
11   I think there are child labor laws that prohibit adults from
12 taking advantage of kids my age. I don't think my parents know
13 about them.
14   I've been keeping track of my hours. Last month, I took
15 care of my brothers for eighteen hours. If I had spent eighteen
16 hours baby-sitting someone else's kids, I'd have enough money
17 to buy that sweater I want. But, no. I'm the unpaid slave labor.
18   I plan to continue keeping track of my time. There's no
19 hope that I'll ever be properly reimbursed for it, but at least I
20 have proof in writing of how I am taken advantage of.
21   Tonight I even have to feed them their dinner, which is a
22 royal pain. P.J.'s idea of fun is to fingerpaint in spaghetti sauce.
23 And Michael refuses to eat anything unless you pour half a
24 bottle of ketchup on it first. He puts ketchup on oatmeal. He
25 puts ketchup on fruit salad. He even makes little sandwiches
26 out of two chocolate chip cookies, with ketchup as the filling.
27 It is totally disgusting to watch my brothers eat.
28   After they have dinner, they're supposed to take a bath.
29 It's necessary to get the spaghetti sauce out of P.J.'s hair and
30 the ketchup out from under Michael's fingernails. Their bath
31 water always looks like someone is bleeding to death.
32   Then I read them stories. Actually, that part of the baby-
33 sitting is fun, because I read them all the books that were my

1   favorites when I was their age.
2   After they go to bed tonight, I get to watch a video that
3   Dad rented for me on his way home. It's one I've been wanting
4   to see. I've already set the clock in the living room ahead a half
5   an hour, so Michael will think it's his bedtime before it really
6   is. That way, I can watch my video sooner.
7   Maybe I can pack my lunch for tomorrow while the
8   monsters play in their dinner. I see Mom remembered to buy
9   my favorite kind of bread and some fresh pears, which I love.
10 It's a good thing I'll have a big lunch tomorrow, since eating
11 dinner with my brothers will spoil my appetite tonight.
12   I'm going to wear my new dress tomorrow, too. Mom
13 finished hemming it today. I really like the material, even
14 though we found it at a half-price sale. We never buy anything
15 unless it's on sale because, to quote my father, "Our budget is
16 rather lean." It's a good thing Mom likes to sew, or I'd probably
17 be going to school naked.
18   If I think about my new dress and my fresh pear and my
19 video while I do brat duty tonight, maybe it won't seem so bad.
20 Still, it really isn't fair for me to have to baby-sit all the time
21 for nothing.
22
23
24
25
26
27
28
29
30
31
32
33
34
35

TEENAGE STRESS

1   I went to the doctor yesterday. I keep breaking out in a
2   rash, like hives, only I'm not allergic to anything and I didn't
3   touch any poisonous plants and I didn't get bit by an insect.
4   The doctor said my rash is caused by stress.
5   When I told my dad, he said, "Stress? What do you have
6   to be stressed about?"
7   I said, "Homework."
8   Dad laughed. According to him, the teen years are the
9   most carefree time of anyone's life. He says I won't know what
10   stress is until I'm an adult and paying my own bills.
11   The truth is, I'm stressed about a lot of things, but home-
12   work is the only one I could mention to my father. For example,
13   I'm stressed because I really like Jennifer Powell and I want
14   to go out with her, but I can't because my best friend, Randy,
15   went out with her a couple of times and he likes her, too. Jen-
16   nifer has let me know she'd like to go out with me, but how can
17   I date her when I know how Randy feels? If I take Jennifer
18   out, Randy will be hurt, and I'll lose a good friend. If I don't
19   take Jennifer out, I'll lose the chance to date someone I really
20   care about. Talk about stress!
21   Then there's the matter of Brian Hagley's cheating. Every
22   time we take a test in math, Brian cheats. Sometimes he looks
23   at my paper and copies down the answers; sometimes he looks
24   at Randy's paper and copies down the answers. If we cover
25   our answers, he peeks at someone else's paper. We have never
26   taken a math test where Brian didn't cheat.
27   My mother and Brian's mother sing in a choral group
28   together. Whenever I go to one of Mom's concerts, Mrs. Hagley
29   says that Brian always speaks highly of me and she's glad he
30   and I are friends. So should I turn him in or not? Would the
31   other kids think I'm a tattletale? Am I doing him a favor to let
32   him get away with cheating?
33   Stress is everywhere. I *breathe* stress when I get up in the

1 morning. I'm trying to find a summer job. Is there anything in
2 the entire world more stressful than applying for a job? My
3 hands sweat so much I can hardly hold the pen to fill out the
4 job application. I have reasonable verbal skills—until I'm talk-
5 ing to a potential employer. Then I have a speech handicap
6 which causes me to blurt out inappropriate responses to crucial
7 questions. For example, I applied for a job at The Fried Chicken
8 Roost. The manager asked me if I had ever bussed dishes, and
9 I said, "No. I always carry them on my bicycle." He smiled
10 politely, but I knew immediately that I would not be working
11 at The Fried Chicken Roost.
12   No wonder I have a rash. I will probably never get a job.
13 When I'm forty-three years old, I will still be filling out job
14 applications at Dairy Queen and McDonalds and making
15 stupid jokes to the proprietors. At least by then, people will
16 admit I have a reason to feel stressed.
17   It is stressful just to be a teen. Adults look at us as if we
18 were dope pushers or delinquents. If I cut my hair different
19 than the older generation, or wear untraditional clothing,
20 adults look away when they see me on the street. They act like
21 being young is a contagious disease even though they all try
22 to look younger.
23   The worst stress of all comes from not knowing who I am.
24 Oh, I know my name and address and who my family is and
25 all of that, but who am I? What do I want to do with my life?
26 What are my goals, besides getting a summer job? What are my
27 talents? What do I want to be doing ten years from now? Will
28 the world be a better place because of me? How?
29   Sometimes I am so full of questions that I think I'll break
30 apart into a thousand pieces. I never do, though. Instead I
31 break out in a thousand little red bumps that itch.
32   The doctor said if I look on the bright side of everything,
33 I wouldn't feel the stress. I tried to figure out what the bright
34 side is. I decided the bright side of teenage stress is this: By
35 the time I'm twenty, I'll outgrow it.

MY MOTHER IS
SIXTEEN YEARS OLD

1   My mother is sixteen years old. Not in *real* years, of course.
2   My mother's true age is thirty-eight, a nice respectable number
3   for a mother to be.

4   Unfortunately, my mom still thinks of herself as sixteen.
5   What's worse, she tries to act that way. If I have a friend over
6   and we're sitting around listening to music and talking, my
7   mom sits with us.

8   Yesterday, my friend, Betsy, was telling me about this new
9   guy she met and how she thinks he might ask her out, and my
10   mom walked in and listened and then she started telling Betsy
11   about a new guy who just got hired at the firm where she works
12   and how she wouldn't be surprised if he asked her out one of
13   these days. It was embarrassing.

14   I do not want a sixteen-year-old mother. I know Mom gets
15   lonely, and I know she doesn't have much time for a social life,
16   but I don't want my friends to be her friends. Don't misun-
17   derstand me; I want Mom to like my friends, and I want them
18   to like her, but that isn't the same as getting all chummy-wummy
19   with them.

20   When I go to Betsy's house, her mother says hello and
21   sometimes talks to me for a minute or two, but that's it. If Betsy's
22   mother has a new man in her life, she keeps the news to herself,
23   and she never asks me personal questions.

24   On the day after the Homecoming Dance, my mom asked
25   Betsy if her date had kissed her. I could have died! Betsy had
26   already told me all about it, but she sure didn't want to tell my
27   mother. She mumbled something under her breath and then
28   Mom launched into a long story about her first kiss.

29   I suppose if I had brothers or sisters, or if Mom and Dad
30   hadn't gotten divorced, it might be different. As it is, it's been
31   just Mom and me for so many years that I guess she's come to
32   depend on me for companionship. Now that I have other people
33   who are important to me, she wants them to be important to

1   her, too. And she wants to be special to them.
2   I don't like to hurt her feelings by asking her to leave my
3   friends and me alone. But it's either that, or my friends are not
4   going to come to my house anymore.
5   Why can't parents grow up gracefully, instead of trying
6   to relive their youth through their kids?
7   I don't want a thirty-eight-year-old pal. I just want a
8   mother.
9
10
11
12
13
14
15
16
17
18
19
20
21
22
23
24
25
26
27
28
29
30
31
32
33
34
35

LETTER FROM CAMP

1   *(This monolog, even when memorized, should be done while*
2   *holding a tablet and pencil, as if you were writing.)*
3
4   Dear Folks: I thought I'd better write to you before you
5   get the hospital bill. Otherwise, you might worry. Mr. Higgins
6   is OK except for the stitches, which will come out next week.
7   Before you start lecturing me about driving when I don't have
8   a license yet, I want to explain that none of it was my fault. Not
9   the fire. Not the loose boa constrictor. And not the garbage can
10 crashing through the window. As you have always told me,
11 there is a logical explanation for everything. You'll be glad to
12 know I am learning you were right about that.
13   You were also right when you said I would like this camp
14 if I would give it half a chance. I was afraid it would be boring.
15 I thought there would be counselors all over the place and
16 strict curfews, and we'd have to do dumb stuff like go on hikes
17 and learn crafts. Boy, was I wrong! Next year, can I sign up
18 for the whole summer instead of just one month? I thought I
19 would be lonesome, but I'm not. Did you know there is a camp
20 for girls just across the river? It only takes twenty minutes to
21 row over there. Even less in daylight.
22   I am getting off the subject; I started to explain about the
23 hospital bill. It all started yesterday afternoon when this guy
24 named Boston said he had found a chain saw and asked if I
25 wanted to help him cut down a tree. I said I had never used a
26 chain saw, but I'd be glad to help since the reason my folks
27 sent me to camp was to learn new skills. By the way, don't you
28 think Boston is a terrific name? He was born while his parents
29 were on a trip to Massachusetts. I said it's a good thing they
30 were not vacationing in New York; they might have named him
31 Buffalo. He said he's always wished they had gone to Min-
32 nesota. People might treat him with more respect if his name
33 was Saint Paul.

1   How would you feel if I changed my name to something
2   more interesting, like Dallas? I think Dallas has a real nice
3   sound and if people think I'm from Texas, so what? Maybe I'll
4   learn to talk with a southern accent. As a matter of fact, I
5   already am.
6   One of the guys in my cabin has a drawl. He's from Atlanta.
7   He says stuff like, "Y'all come see me, hea?" At first I had a
8   hard time understanding him, but now that I'm used to it I like
9   his accent. A drawl has more character than ordinary speech.
10   It is also contagious. Do not be surprised if I have a drawl when
11   I come home, even though this camp is not in the south. When
12   you live in the same cabin with someone who says "y'all," it's
13   nearly impossible not to say it, too.
14   His name is Jem, and he taught us how to cook cajun hot
15   dogs. You'll be happy to know that I am no longer a picky eater.
16   All those reminders you gave me about tasting everything once,
17   even if it's not what we eat at home, must have had some effect
18   on my subconscious mind because I've eaten lots of stuff we
19   never had at home. It's all been at night, not during regular
20   meals, but what's the difference as long as I'm learning to like
21   a variety of food? My favorite, besides the cajun hot dogs, is
22   something called Gut Buster's Orgy. It's made with crushed
23   potato chips, maple syrup, dill pickles, melted chocolate bars,
24   peanut butter, ketchup, raisins, and a couple of other things I
25   can't remember. I'll try to write down the recipe so I can make
26   it for you when I get home. Maybe I'll make it for Grandma's
27   birthday, since she's always saying if I learned how to cook I
28   wouldn't be so picky. The dentist that Mr. Higgins took me to
29   says I'll have the new caps on my teeth before I go home, so I
30   will be able to chew some Gut Buster's Orgy on both sides of
31   my mouth again. Maybe for Grandma I will call it something
32   more delicate, like Tummy Tickler's Delight, even though orgy
33   is one of my new words. I have become very aware of language
34   since I got here. In fact, my vocabulary is growing rapidly.
35   Some of the words I never heard before. Some I had wondered

1   about because I saw them written in public places, but I didn't
2   want to bother you by asking what they meant. Well, now I
3   know, which should make you happy since you are always
4   saying I should expand my mind.
5   I hope you are OK and not too lonely with the house all
6   to yourselves. I am fine, as you can tell from this newsy letter,
7   which I am sure you did not expect but, as I said at the start,
8   I didn't want you to worry about me. I'll try to write again soon.
9   I just realized I haven't told you about the poison yet, but that
10   will have to wait until my next letter because the sheriff just
11   got here and I am one of the people who has to testify.
12   Your loving son, Dallas.
13   P.S. Don't try to call. The electricity and telephone lines
14   are still dead from when the tree fell the wrong way. Boston
15   had never used a chain saw before, either.
16
17
18
19
20
21
22
23
24
25
26
27
28
29
30
31
32
33
34
35

MY FATHER
NEVER HUGGED ME

1   If I ever have a kid of my own, I'm going to be a lot different
2 with him than my parents are to me. If my kid wants me to play
3 catch with him, I'll never say, "Not now. Can't you see I'm busy?"
4   If my kid doesn't like carrots, I'll never make him sit at
5 the table until he eats at least one spoonful.
6   If my kid is talking to his friend on the telephone, I won't
7 butt in after only ten minutes and tap my finger on my watch
8 to signal that he has to hang up now.
9   And I'll hug my kid at least once a day. My father has
10 never hugged me. When I was little, he didn't hug me when he
11 put me to bed or when he left to go to work or when he came
12 home. Not even when I was two years old and fell down the
13 front steps and cracked my head on the sidewalk.
14   Whenever I tried to crawl into his lap, he pushed me away
15 and told me to go play with my trucks. When I got older, if I
16 tried to put my arm around his shoulder, he shrugged me off
17 and said, "None of that sissy stuff."
18   I remember asking him to read me a story once and when
19 he said he would, I sat down on the sofa next to him, snuggling
20 as close as I could. He moved away. I felt like I must have little
21 crawly green germs that would travel from my body to his if
22 he wasn't cautious.
23   My friend, Jeff, says his father never hugs him, either, but
24 he doesn't care. Jeff says he wishes his mom and his Aunt
25 Esther would quit trying to hug him so much. He says getting
26 hugged by Aunt Esther is like being smothered with a huge
27 feather pillow.
28   When I was four, I got a stuffed elephant for my birthday.
29 I named him Peanuts, and I carried him everywhere. Every
30 night, I fell asleep with my arms around Peanuts, hugging him
31 as tight as I could. Somehow, hugging Peanuts every night
32 made up for not getting any hugs in the daytime. We moved
33 when I was ten. As I was unpacking my things in the new

1   apartment, I couldn't find Peanuts. I asked Mom if she knew
2   where he was packed, and she said, "That old moth-eaten
3   elephant? I threw it out. You're too old for such baby toys."
4   That's another thing I'll never do to my kid. I'll never
5   throw anything of his away without asking him first.
6   If someone gives him money for his birthday, I'll let him
7   spend it on anything he wants. I'll never make him put it in a
8   savings account. If he wants to blow the whole thing on candy
9   or video games at the mall, I'll let him. And when it's all gone
10   and he has nothing to show for it, I'll never say, "I told you so."
11   To be fair, I should tell you that my parents have done a
12   lot for me. They sent me to camp every summer. They paid for
13   trombone lessons. I had a swing set and a tricycle and, later,
14   a ten-speed. I hope I can give my kid those expensive things,
15   too, but even if I can't, I know I'll hug him a lot.
16   I'll always hug him a lot.
17
18
19
20
21
22
23
24
25
26
27
28
29
30
31
32
33
34
35

IT'S NOT MY FAULT

1   I get blamed for everything around here. If there was a
2 tornado and the roof blew off our house and landed in Mexico,
3 my family would probably say it was my fault. They'd say I
4 should have realized the shingles were loose and nailed them
5 down tighter.
6   No matter what happens, my parents point their fingers
7 at me. I will give you an example. Last Saturday, I was supposed
8 to mow the lawn. My parents went grocery shopping, and they
9 said the lawn had better be mowed when they got home. Or else.
10   They never say or else what. They say, "Or else." I've never
11 had the nerve to find out what "or else" means.
12   At any rate, they went off to the grocery store and I, being
13 the dutiful kid that I am, went out to the garage to get out the
14 lawn mower. As I passed my father's workbench, I noticed that
15 the bird house he is building was nearly finished. It's really
16 more of a bird condominium, with several separate entrances.
17 He sawed and sanded for weeks and then spent more weeks
18 painting it white with a decorative green trim. He even painted
19 little names over the holes. "Mrs. Robin" and "The Sparrow
20 Family."
21   Unfortunately, when I leaned over the bird house to ad-
22 mire it more closely, I bumped the upper shelf and knocked
23 off a can of red paint, which opened and splattered all over the
24 bird house. It was as if that bird house had developed a sudden
25 case of measles.
26   I grabbed a rag and tried to wipe the paint off, but all it
27 did was smear. Then I got some paint thinner and dabbed it
28 on the spots. The paint thinner took off the red paint, but it
29 also removed everything underneath it, right down to the bare
30 wood.
31   I knew I was in big trouble. My only hope was to repaint
32 the whole birdhouse before my dad got home. It wasn't easy.
33 The biggest problem was that when I put fresh white paint over

1 the red dots, the red wasn't quite dry yet, so the bird house
2 ended up being pink.
3   I had just finished washing out the brush when my folks
4 drove up. The first thing they noticed was the long grass. I
5 couldn't tell them the real reason why I had not mowed the
6 lawn so I said Skipper, our dog, had wanted to go out so I took
7 him for a long walk on his leash. Skipper makes a good excuse
8 because he will never contradict anything I say about him.
9   I got out the mower but before I even started it, my mother
10 flagged me down and said she had just had a telephone call
11 from Eric's mother. Eric had confessed that he and I were the
12 ones who broke Mrs. Smithson's front window.
13   Here is what happened: Eric and I were sitting on his front
14 steps, swapping baseball cards, when we heard a pitiful meow-
15 ing. There was a kitten on Mrs. Smithson's roof. The poor thing
16 looked half-starved, and it clearly did not know how to get
17 down. Eric and I both knew we had to help that poor little cat.
18   I got a ladder. Eric held it steady while I climbed up. The
19 kitten wouldn't come to me. Finally I got on the roof and chased
20 it. Eric climbed up the ladder. I caught the kitten and tried to
21 hand it to Eric, but the kitten clawed my arm and I yelled and
22 dropped it on Eric's head, and he screamed and jumped and
23 the ladder went crashing through the window. The broken glass
24 set off Mrs. Smithson's burglar alarm. Eric and I were afraid
25 we'd get arrested for breaking in. He put the ladder back up,
26 I climbed off the roof, and we hightailed it for home. Later,
27 when I was asked if I had seen anyone break that window, I
28 said no, which was the truth. How could I see it when I was
29 way up on the roof?
30   I couldn't believe that Eric had blabbed. My mother
31 marched me over to Mrs. Smithson to apologize and to say that
32 I would pay for the window out of my allowance. Mrs. Smithson
33 came to the door, but before I could say one word, she snapped,
34 "It's about time you got here. That dog has been harrassing my
35 poor little cat all morning." It seems she had called our house

1 several times to complain that Skipper was over in her yard. I
2 didn't hear the phone because I was out in the garage. My
3 mother didn't ask me how Skipper could be chasing Mrs.
4 Smithson's cat while I was walking him on his leash, but she
5 gave me a look that let me know I was about to find out what
6 "or else" means.
7 We calmed Mrs. Smithson down and took Skipper home.
8 I planned to explain how the window was not my fault.
9 The unmowed lawn was not my fault. But I had barely begun
10 when I heard my father let out a war whoop in the garage. He
11 had just seen his pink birdhouse. He did not even ask me if I
12 had done it; he just started yelling at me.
13 Like I said, I get blamed for everything around here.
14
15
16
17
18
19
20
21
22
23
24
25
26
27
28
29
30
31
32
33
34
35

13

FIRST AND LAST
BABY-SITTING JOB

1   Last night I had my first baby-sitting job. It will also be
2   my last baby-sitting job. I've been wanting to baby-sit for a
3   year but, until yesterday, nobody asked me. Then Mrs. Bride-
4   man, who knows my parents, called and asked Mom if I ever
5   did any baby-sitting. She had an important meeting and her
6   usual sitter had cancelled.
7   After Mom agreed to let me do it, she gave me a ten-minute
8   lecture about being responsible. I promised not to use the Bride-
9   mans' phone unless it was an emergency and not to eat anything
10   unless Mrs. Brideman specifically said I could and not to let
11   Willie Brideman out of my sight for one second.
12   Since the Bridemans live only three blocks from us, I
13   walked over. On my way, I saw a kid named Jerry Hooper who
14   is a couple of grades ahead of me. He was riding his bike. He
15   asked me where I was going and I told him, and he said he
16   lives two doors down from the Bridemans.
17   I didn't talk anymore because I didn't want to be late to
18   my first job, and besides, I haven't had much experience talking
19   to boys outside of school, especially older ones, and it made
20   me nervous.
21   I just got Willie in his pajamas and was reading him a
22   story when someone knocked on the door. "Who is it?" I asked.
23   It was Jerry. Jerry Hooper. I opened the door and asked
24   him what he wanted, and he said he had come to visit me. Willie
25   said, "Hi, Jerry."
26   I said I didn't think he should come in when Mrs. Brideman
27   wasn't home, but Jerry claimed he visited the Bridemans all
28   the time. I wondered why Mrs. Brideman had not asked Jerry
29   to babysit, instead of calling me.
30   "Did Mrs. Brideman say you couldn't have company?"
31   Jerry asked. I admitted she had not said that. Willie ran and
32   got his ball and handed it to Jerry, but I told him that Jerry
33   wasn't coming in.

1   Willie started to cry. Jerry stepped inside and told him
2   not to cry, that he would play ball with him. Jerry picked up
3   the ball and tossed it. Willie tried to throw it back. It hit a lamp
4   and knocked it over. The lamp shattered. Willie *really* cried
5   then. It was past his bedtime, and nothing I could do or say
6   calmed him down. Finally, I put him in his highchair and gave
7   him a bowl of ice cream. He yowled harder.

8   Jerry and I were trying to sweep up the broken glass when
9   Mrs. Brideman came home. Willie was still screaming. By then,
10   I wasn't sure if he was crying over the broken lamp or because
11   the ice cream felt cold in his hair. Mrs. Brideman told Jerry to
12   leave, picked Willie up and comforted him, and informed me
13   that she would never ask me to baby-sit again. Worst of all, she
14   called my mom and said that I had invited my boyfriend over
15   while she was gone. Mom ranted and raved like I had tied Willie
16   Brideman to a chair and tortured him. She didn't even want to
17   hear my side of what had happened.

18   The next day, after she had calmed down a little, Mom
19   said she didn't know I had a boyfriend. I told her I don't. I said
20   Mrs. Brideman jumped to the wrong conclusion, based on cir-
21   cumstantial evidence. Then I explained exactly what had hap-
22   pened. Well, Mom got angry all over again, only this time she
23   wasn't mad at me, she was mad at Jerry for going in the house
24   after I told him not to and at Mrs. Brideman for assuming I
25   had invited him.

26   I feel better about the whole mess now that Mom is on my
27   side. I know one thing: If I ever get another baby-sitting job,
28   which seems unlikely, I will lock the door and refuse to open
29   it no matter who is on the other side.

30
31
32
33
34
35

REMEMBERING BOO-BOO

1   The oddest things remind me of Boo-Boo. For instance,
2 the ocean. Boo-Boo was such a little dog and the ocean is so
3 vast—yet I can never walk along the beach without seeing in
4 my memory a small, black dog, skimming along the sand with
5 his tail streaming out behind him.

6   He never actually went in the water. I think he was secretly
7 afraid of the waves, although he would growl and bark fiercely
8 at them if they came too close. Watching him race along the
9 shore, I always felt free, too, as if all the invisible leashes that
10 restrain me had been, for a short time, removed.

11   I remember Boo-Boo on hot summer days, when I abandon
12 the mower and take a quick nap in a lawn chair. Boo-Boo's
13 attitude about naps was straightforward. To him, they were
14 necessities, not luxuries, particularly if the nap could be taken
15 in the sun. In winter, he made do with patches of sun coming
16 through the windows, which necessitated frequent moves in
17 order to stay on a bright patch of carpet. In summer, he snored
18 grandly in a lawn chair. He got so warm, we nicknamed him
19 The Black Panter, but he never wanted to sleep in the shade.

20   I had an argument with my best friend last week and,
21 oddly, that also reminded me of Boo-Boo. I didn't have to scold
22 Boo-Boo often, but when I did, he was devastated, slinking
23 about with his head down and his tail between his legs, looking
24 mournful. He always wanted to make up as quickly as possible.
25 If I ignored him, he crept toward me, tail wagging tentatively,
26 and licked my shoe. How can you stay mad at someone who's
27 willing to lick your shoe? After John and I quarreled, we didn't
28 talk to each other for two days. Then I decided I would be like
29 Boo-Boo and make the first move, regardless of who was at
30 fault. Instead of staying away, I walked up to John and said I
31 missed him and wanted to be friends again. He grinned and
32 gave me a hug and said he was sure glad to hear that.

33   Come to think of it, Boo-Boo knew the right thing to do

1   in lots of situations. When I had the flu and thought my stomach
2   was going to turn inside out, my folks tried to cheer me up with
3   a lot of chatter about how I would feel better soon. Boo-Boo
4   just lay quietly beside me, as if to say, "I'm here if you need
5   me, but I won't bother you." I remembered that when my uncle
6   had cancer surgery. I went to the hospital and sat in the lobby
7   for five hours. I didn't bother anyone; I just sat there. Later,
8   my aunt thanked me about ten times and said it was a great
9   comfort to her to know that if she wanted someone to talk to,
10   I was there. "How did you know exactly the right thing to do?"
11   she asked. I just shrugged; I didn't tell her Boo-Boo taught me.
12   When the neighborhood gang used to play hide-and-seek,
13   I always had to shut Boo-Boo in the house. Otherwise, he gave
14   away my hiding place. No matter where I hid, Boo-Boo would
15   sniff me out and then dance exuberantly in front of my hiding
16   place. He couldn't holler, "I spy," but he sure knew a lot about
17   nonverbal communication.
18   Boo-Boo was already five years old when I was born. He
19   was a part of my life for twelve years. When people said I was
20   an only child, my folks always shook their heads and said,
21   "Don't forget Boo-Boo."
22   I won't ever forget Boo-Boo. We shared a bed, and count-
23   less games of tuggy-rag, and more than one Girl Scout cookie.
24   From him, I learned about trust and loyalty and when to keep
25   my mouth shut. I learned that a mixed heritage can produce a
26   sterling personality. I learned that enthusiasm gets results and
27   forgiveness is better than sulking. I learned it's more important
28   to have someone who loves you than it is to always win the
29   game. And I learned that, for every creature, there is a time
30   for living and a time for dying.
31   Boo-Boo taught me one other thing: There is no end to
32   love, because happy memories remain forever in the heart.
33   You can't ask much more than that of a dog.
34
35

15

FREE ICE CREAM
ALL SUMMER

1   Last May, the local ice cream store had a special promo-
2 tion. Every time anyone bought an ice cream cone during the
3 month of May, they got a little red ticket with a number on it.
4 There was a drawing scheduled, and the winning number
5 would get free ice cream for the whole summer. Two quarts
6 per week for three months.

7   I imagined a glorious summer, pigging out on free ice
8 cream. What bliss! What ecstasy! I daydreamed about it for a
9 whole month, seeing myself with huge bowls heaped with
10 Blackberry Marble or Triple Chocolate Fudge Delight. It nearly
11 happened, too. In fact, it should have happened. If I didn't have
12 a traitor for a sister, it *would* have happened.

13   My sister, Bev, and I bought a lot of ice cream cones during
14 May, to get as many tickets as we could. Each time, Bev ordered
15 first because she always knew what she wanted and I didn't.
16 She got Banana Walnut every time, which I thought showed
17 lack of originality and poor taste. Banana Walnut is the only
18 kind of ice cream I don't like.

19   While Bev got her Banana Walnut cone, I would read the
20 list of flavors and peer through the glass freezer top at the open
21 containers of ice cream and try to decide. Because she always
22 went first, Bev's number each time was one digit before mine.
23 If she got number 15, I had number 16. When she got number
24 43, I got 44.

25   The drawing was held June first. When I got home from
26 my paper route that day, Bev was waiting for me. I've never
27 seen her so excited. "You won!" she screamed, before I was
28 even in the house. "We get free ice cream all summer."

29   "How do you know?" I asked.

30   Bev said she went to the ice cream store to see if the win-
31 ning number had been selected. There was a big sign in the
32 window: Number 114 Wins Free Ice Cream All Summer. Bev
33 said she ran home and looked at all her tickets and when she

1   came to number 113, she knew that I had the winner because

2   I always got the next number after hers.

3   I jumped around, grinning and shaking my hands in the

4   air. I even hugged my sister. I was going to have all the Straw-

5   berry, Pistachio, and Almond-Butter-Crunch ice cream I could

6   eat. Maybe I would get a different flavor every week for the

7   entire summer. I'd been wanting to try Licorice/Marshmallow

8   and Peanut Butter Broccoli.

9   Bev said, "All you have to do is take ticket number 114

10   down to the store and turn it in, and we are in ice cream heaven

11   for the next three months." She emphasized the word *we*.

12   I quit jumping and grinning. I said, "What do you mean,

13   I have to turn in the ticket?"

14   Bev gave me the look that she always gives me when she

15   thinks I'm acting like a retarded two-year-old. "Of course you

16   have to turn in the winning number," she said. "How else does

17   the ice cream store know you're the one who has it?"

18   At that moment, I felt exactly the way I did when the

19   dentist announced I needed braces. I looked at my shoes and

20   kept my mouth shut. My dismay must have been obvious be-

21   cause Bev said, "Don't tell me you didn't keep your numbers.

22   Oh, no! Even you can't be that stupid." When I didn't reply, she

23   continued: "You threw them away, didn't you?" I nodded mis-

24   erably. She said, "And the garbage got picked up yesterday.

25   Free ice cream for the entire summer and my idiot brother

26   throws it away."

27   Bev can get worked into quite a froth when she gets

28   started. I decided not to stick around and watch. I told her I

29   didn't save the numbers on purpose. "Ice cream," I informed

30   her, "is not on my improved low-fat nutrition plan for the sum-

31   mer. Even if I had the winning ticket, I would not turn it in."

32   That wasn't true, of course, but it made me feel better to say

33   it. Mustering every shred of dignity I could, I stomped away.

34   An hour later, as I sat on the back porch debating whether

35   to cry or make popcorn, Bev joined me. She had a quart of

1   Banana Walnut ice cream and a spoon. She was gobbling it
2   straight from the carton.
3   When I asked her where she got the money for a whole
4   quart of ice cream, she told me it was free. The way she said
5   it made me suspicious. I knew she was setting me up, but I was
6   too curious not to ask *how* she got a free quart of ice cream.
7   "I thought about you throwing away all your tickets," she
8   said, "and it dawned on me that you might not have thrown
9   them in the garbage. Maybe they went in the recycle box. So I
10 dumped all the paper out of the recycle box and rummaged
11 around, and what do you think I found? Ticket number 114."
12   I glared at her. Number 114 was *my* ticket.
13   She said, "I knew you didn't want it, since ice cream is not
14 on your improved low-fat nutrition plan for the summer, so I
15 turned it in myself. I got to choose which flavors I want. I signed
16 up for two quarts of Banana Walnut every week for three whole
17 months. This is the first one." She dipped her spoon into the
18 container and said, "It's going to be a wonderful summer."
19   Bev was wrong.
20   It was a terrible summer.
21
22
23
24
25
26
27
28
29
30
31
32
33
34
35

FAMILY TALK

1   Sometimes I feel as if I live under a microscope. Every
2 word I say, and every action I take, is carefully examined by
3 my parents. Even worse, they tell other people all about me. I
4 have no secrets.
5   For the first few years of my life, I thought I was invisible.
6 My parents discussed me with other people as if I wasn't there,
7 while I stood right in front of them. They would never do that
8 to another adult. I vividly remember my mother and my Aunt
9 June talking about the cute things I did and said. I loved hear-
10 ing them tell how cute I was. It made me want to do those same
11 things over and over.
12   Just as vividly, I remember my mother and my grand-
13 mother discussing how naughty I was. Mother listed everything
14 I had done in recent weeks that I should not have done. I jumped
15 on the sofa. I pulled the cat's tail. I carried my juice into the
16 living room and spilled it. Instead of taking a nap, I stripped
17 all the blankets and sheets off my crib and threw them on the
18 floor. I put Cheerios in the dishwasher. On and on it went. Most
19 of the complaints were about things I didn't know were wrong
20 until after I had done them. Even though my mother laughed
21 as she told Grandma all this, I felt diminished, as if I had a
22 serious character flaw, when I heard my mother relating all of
23 my mistakes.
24   Eventually, my parents caught on that I was not deaf and
25 that I was capable of understanding what they said about me.
26 Then they started to spell. They said things like, "(Name) put
27 an A-P-P-L-E down the T-O-I-L-E-T." I knew, of course, that
28 they were discussing me, since they never bothered to spell out
29 my name. This left me wondering what was so terrible, so hor-
30 rible, that they could not talk about it in front of me. I imagined
31 my parents were getting a divorce. I thought my older brother
32 was dying. I thought the dog had been stolen. It took several
33 weeks of these spelled-out conversations, with no unhappy

1   occurrences in the family, before I caught on that they were
2   merely talking about me, as they always had, but in a different
3   way.
4   When I learned to spell, Mother resorted to whispering.
5   She would wait until I was in the next room, lower her voice,
6   and talk fast. One day, I charged into the living room and yelled,
7   "If Grandma wants to know what I've been doing, I'll tell her.
8   You don't need to whisper about me when I'm in the kitchen."
9   Mother looked shocked. It was as if it never dawned on
10   her that I didn't like being gossiped about. Since that day, the
11   problem hasn't been quite so bad. I'm sure my parents still
12   discuss me when I'm not there, but at least they don't do it
13   anymore when I'm present.
14   When I think how my private business has been spread
15   all over town by my parents, it makes me furious. Mother tells
16   my aunt and my grandma. My dad tells my uncle. Sometimes
17   they both tell the people they work with, too. It's disloyal! When
18   I ran my bike into a tree, everyone knew. When I fell asleep on
19   the school bus and rode all the way to the bus barn, everyone
20   knew. When I baked cookies and mistakenly used powdered
21   mushroom instead of cinnamon, my mother could hardly wait
22   to get on the phone.
23   What someone does in the privacy of their own home
24   should not be discussed with other people, no matter how in-
25   teresting it is, without that person's permission. I would never
26   tell my friends the everyday things my mother and father do,
27   no matter how funny or annoying they are. *(Slight pause)*
28   Or would I? I guess that's what I am doing right now.
29
30
31
32
33
34
35

SLUG SLIME
AND OTHER ENDEARMENTS

1   My friend, Alexander, complains because he doesn't have
2   a nickname. He's an only child and his parents have always
3   called him Alexander, rather than Alex or Al. He says it's too
4   formal. He says he wants to be PeeWee or Spike or something
5   else that's completely unrelated to Alexander.
6   In my opinion, Alexander doesn't know how lucky he is.
7   I'll bet it's been at least two years since any of my brothers
8   have called me by my real name. They always call me things like
9   Elephant Ears or Toe Jam or Diaper Delinquent. I told Alexan-
10   der he was welcome to use any of the nicknames that my
11   brothers call me, anytime he wants them. I told him he could
12   choose from such gems as Ugly Face or Stink Bomb.
13   I've noticed that the names my brothers have for me are
14   always two part. One word would be bad enough; I always get
15   double whammies like Big Bottom or Garlic Breath or Jelly
16   Belly.
17   I used to complain to my mother, but she always refused
18   to get involved. She claims that family nicknames are actually
19   expressions of endearment and should not be taken literally. I
20   asked her how she could possibly believe that Slug Slime was
21   an expression of endearment, but she just laughed and told me
22   it was a good example of alliteration.
23   To her credit, I admit she refuses to get involved when
24   my brothers complain to her about me, too. Not that they ever
25   have anything serious to complain about.
26   It wouldn't be so bad to go through life being called Fanny
27   Flab or Pimple Puss if they would confine their remarks to our
28   own house. But, no. My brothers like nothing better than to
29   call me revolting names in front of my friends. It's disgusting.
30   The other day, I was standing in front of the school talking
31   to Merilee Putnam, who is the cutest girl in my entire grade
32   and who had never before until that very moment noticed that
33   I was alive. Merilee had just asked me if she could look at my

1   history notes from the week she was sick, when one of my
2   brothers went past. Now, any normal sibling, given such cir-
3   cumstances, would simply smile and keep going. Better yet,
4   they would notice that I was a nervous wreck in the middle of
5   the most important conversation of my life and pretend not to
6   recognize me.
7   Not my brother. He grinned and said, "Hey, Liver Lips.
8   How about introducing me to your friend?" Merilee just
9   laughed, but I could have shot him.
10   I told Alexander about it the next day. I repeated how
11   lucky he was not to have a bunch of bratty brothers to embar-
12   rass him with stupid nicknames.
13   There goes one of my brothers now. I guess I'll walk home
14   with him. *(Yells.)* Hey, Garbage Odor! Wait for me! *(He exits.)*
15
16
17
18
19
20
21
22
23
24
25
26
27
28
29
30
31
32
33
34
35

MY HEAD IS FULL
OF STARSHINE

1   My friend, Pam, says my head is full of starshine. She
2   laughs when she says it. What she really means is that she
3   doesn't always understand the poems I write, but she's glad
4   that I write them. She means she recognizes that I'm not like
5   her, but it's OK for me to be different.
6   Pam is practical. Every night before she goes to sleep,
7   Pam makes a list of what she needs to do the next day. She
8   puts down items like return library books and hem dress for
9   Margo's party on Saturday. When the list is made, she numbers
10   the items in order of importance. If it's critical, it's Number
11   One. Pam has never had to pay an overdue fine at the library
12   and when Saturday arrives, her dress will not only be hemmed,
13   it will be washed, ironed, and ready to wear.
14   I have a long history of library fines. Twenty cents here,
15   fifty cents there. I'm always amazed to notice that a book is
16   overdue. It just never seems like three weeks could go by so
17   quickly. When Saturday comes, I'll be rummaging frantically
18   through my closet, hoping to find something decent to wear to
19   the party. But I wrote a birthday poem for Margo that I like a
20   lot. It took me two days; I think Margo will like it, too.
21   My mother often wonders aloud why I can't be more like
22   Pam. Just once, according to my mother, it would be nice to
23   know more than twenty-four hours in advance that your child
24   is performing in a school concert. I always forget to bring home
25   the notices, or else I write something on the back and stick
26   them in my desk. Either way, Mom doesn't get them in time to
27   make plans.
28   On my last report card, Mr. Evans, my science teacher,
29   wrote that I am not working up to my potential. He said I tend
30   to daydream, instead of paying attention in class. I have to
31   admit that's true, especially when we were learning about in-
32   sects. Pam found the unit on insects fascinating. Too fascinat-
33   ing, if you ask me. One day she sat beside me in the cafeteria

1   and announced that ladybugs eat aphids, spider mites, white-
2   flies and mealybugs.
3   I said, "Yuck."
4   Pam continued blissfully on, informing me that ladybugs
5   eat several times their own weight in insects every day. I put
6   down my peanut butter sandwich and told Pam that the conver-
7   sation was not very appetizing, but she was so excited about
8   ladybugs that she didn't even hear me. She just babbled on
9   about how even the ladybug larvae eat insects and how a com-
10   pany in California collects the ladybugs and sells them to fruit
11   growers, to eat the aphids off the fruit trees. I finally moved to
12   a different table, but by then my appetite was gone.
13   Pam got an A in science. I only get As in English. Some
14   kids moan and complain whenever they have to write an essay
15   or a story, but I love assignments like that. I have a whole
16   notebook full of ideas for stories and poems that I intend to
17   write someday. I also have a list of good titles. My favorite title
18   is "Magic Mud in Kansas City," but so far I haven't been able
19   to think of a story to go with it.
20   I will, though. I always do. Usually it happens when I least
21   expect it, like when I'm sitting in science class trying not to get
22   sick as I listen to how certain animals eat their young. When
23   Mr. Evans talks about gross things like that, I pretend my chair
24   is a flying carpet, and I watch myself float out the window, up
25   past the flagpole and over the trees. Sometimes I pretend that
26   I fly beyond the moon, to a different galaxy, where I meet won-
27   derful creatures with purple beards who ride on giant rabbits.
28   Maybe Pam is right. My head is full of starshine. Except
29   for those library fines, I'm glad it is.
30
31
32
33
34
35

19

NINTENDO HUMILIATION

1   Yesterday was absolutely the most mortifying day of my
2   entire life. I was so embarrassed! And my own father caused
3   the whole awful episode. Can you imagine a parent who is so
4   unmerciful that he would humiliate his son in front of an entire
5   group of people?
6   Here is what happened:
7   I was in my fifth period math class, which is taught by
8   Mrs. Kipler, when someone knocked on the door. I should point
9   out that math is not my strongest subject. I used to be good in
10   math. In fact, I used to get mostly As and an occasional B in
11   math. That was before this year, before I got Mrs. Kipler.
12   Don't get me wrong. I like Mrs. Kipler. She's an OK lady,
13   and she has a sense of humor. She's even a good teacher. The
14   problem is, she gives homework assignments every day, and I
15   just don't have time to do all that homework. When I get home
16   from school, I need to relax.
17   For the last few months, my relaxation has been Nintendo.
18   I got my Nintendo at about the same time I started math with
19   Mrs. Kipler.
20   I am good at Nintendo. You might even say I excel at
21   Nintendo. If everyone has a natural talent, mine is Nintendo.
22   Unfortunately, I found it impossible to excel at Nintendo
23   and to excel at math at the same time. Both require my time
24   and attention after school.
25   The conflict came to light when I got my report card. When
26   my father saw the D-minus in math, he asked me what was
27   wrong. I explained about Mrs. Kipler and the daily homework
28   assignments. Dad nodded and said nothing.
29   I said, "I simply do not have time for all that math
30   homework."
31   Dad nodded and said nothing. I was astonished. I expected
32   him to be a thunderstorm, glowering and rumbling for hours,
33   drenching me with accusations and threats. Instead, he just sat

1   there, calm and quiet as summer sunshine.

2   Lightning struck the next day. Like I said, I was sitting in
3   Mrs. Kipler's fifth period math class when someone knocked
4   on the door. It was my father. He carried my Nintendo.

5   "Hello," he said to Mrs. Kipler, sounding as cheerful as if
6   he had come to hand out candy bars. "I'm *(Name)*'s father, and
7   I've brought you his Nintendo."

8   My mouth fell open as I saw Dad hand my Nintendo to
9   my teacher.

10   "I want you to keep it for him," Dad said, "until his grades
11   improve."

12   "Oh, good," said Mrs. Kipler. "I'll take it home and play
13   with it."

14   The other kids roared with laughter. You never heard
15   such a commotion. You would have thought my father was the
16   stand-up comic of the year. I wanted to slither out of my seat
17   and slink away, but of course I had to sit there while the entire
18   fifth-period math class pointed at me and hooted with laughter.

19   "You can decide when to give it back," Dad said. Then he
20   smiled at Mrs. Kipler, nodded to me, and left.

21   Somehow, I lived through the rest of the day. When I got
22   home that afternoon, I was lost without my Nintendo. I wan-
23   dered through the house, feeling as if someone had died. There
24   was nothing to do. I wasn't even hungry, which proves how
25   traumatized I was. Eventually, I got so bored I did my math
26   homework.

27   All of this happened six weeks ago. Yesterday we got re-
28   port cards again. I got a B-plus in math. I also got my Nintendo
29   back. Mrs. Kipler said she had not played with it, after all.

30   I took it home and, as soon as I finished my homework, I
31   played for three straight hours. I'm happy to say I still have
32   my talent. I still excel at Nintendo.

33   I'm pretty good at math, too.

34

35

20

GRANDMA THINKS
I'M BEAUTIFUL

1   My grandma thinks I am beautiful. She can look straight
2 at my flabby thighs and my frizzed hair and my knobby knees
3 and still believe I'm the most gorgeous person alive.
4   Sometimes I tease her about it. I say, "Grandma, is some-
5 thing wrong with your eyesight? Have you had your glasses
6 checked recently? There are two huge pimples on my nose,
7 glowing like red lanterns. My ears are completely out of pro-
8 portion to the rest of my head; they look like a pair of deformed
9 mushrooms growing from the sides of my face. I would let my
10 hair grow out to cover my ears except every hair on my head
11 has a split end."
12   And do you know how she responds? Grandma laughs and
13 says, "To me, you are beautiful. And don't you ever forget it."
14   Secretly, I'm glad that she has never let me talk her out
15 of her opinion. It's comforting to know that no matter how ugly
16 I am to the rest of the world, there's at least one person who
17 thinks I look great. The funny thing is, when I'm with her, I
18 *feel* more beautiful. I stand up straighter and keep my hair
19 combed and wear clean clothes. Since she believes so hard that
20 I am beautiful, I feel an obligation to at least try to live up to
21 her expectations.
22   It isn't just my looks that Grandma applauds. It's every-
23 thing about me. She says I'm smart. She's constantly amazed at
24 the clever things I do. According to Grandma, I am well ahead
25 of any other kid my age in reasoning ability, athletic skill and
26 conversational artistry. To say nothing of my musical talent.
27   The truth is, I am average. I'm good at some things, not
28 so good at others. If they had a universal curve for kids, overall
29 I guess I'd place right about in the middle. Grandma would
30 never admit that for a minute. She has always believed, and
31 no doubt will continue to believe, that I'm right off the charts.
32 Top dog. The genius kid of all time whose sterling character
33 and sparkling personality match her sensational IQ.

1   Amazingly, she doesn't brag about me to her friends. Maybe
2 she's afraid that if she started in on how clever I am, they would
3 all want equal time to talk about their grandchildren.
4   She doesn't need to tell anyone else how she feels about
5 me. The important thing is that she always lets *me* know how
6 special I am: How bright and funny. How kind and fair. How
7 honest and courageous. How beautiful.
8   Sometimes when I feel lazy and don't want to do my best
9 at a difficult task, I think about Grandma and I try a bit harder.
10 If I'm tempted to say something mean, I remember how good
11 it feels to get a compliment, so I say something nice instead.
12 When I think how proud Grandma will be if I do well in school,
13 I'm never tempted to cheat or skip a test or neglect my home-
14 work. When you have a first-rate cheering squad, it makes you
15 want to win the game. I don't ever want Grandma to be disap-
16 pointed in me or ashamed of anything I do.
17   Every kid—and every adult—should have someone in
18 their life who thinks they're beautiful. Most people would
19 accomplish more and be happier, as well, if they could have
20 my grandma, or someone like her, who firmly believes that they
21 are wonderful and smart and kind.
22   Although I tease her about her eyesight and tell her she
23 is hallucinating, I'm glad my grandma thinks I am beautiful.
24   I think she's beautiful, too.
25
26
27
28
29
30
31
32
33
34
35

Dialogs

THE SLAVE

1   *CAST:*   Two female players, Maggie and Laura.

2   *SETTING:*   Optional.

3

4   *(MAGGIE and LAURA enter.)*

5   MAGGIE: Do you want to come over on Saturday? We could

6   do my new aerobics video and make brownies.

7   LAURA: I can't. Jason has a softball game.

8   MAGGIE: What time is his game?

9   LAURA: It starts at ten, but it's a double-header so we'll be

10   there all day.

11   MAGGIE: What do you do while he plays softball?

12   LAURA: Watch.

13   MAGGIE: All day? It sounds boring.

14   LAURA: It is. I mean, I like to watch him play, but there's

15   nobody to talk to and sometimes the games go on and on

16   forever.

17   MAGGIE: Come over to my house instead. I guarantee: no

18   boredom.

19   LAURA: Jason really wants me to go to all his games.

20   MAGGIE: Why? You don't sit with him, do you?

21   LAURA: Oh, no. If there are bleachers, I sit there. Otherwise,

22   I just sit in the grass.

23   MAGGIE: Since you don't actually spend the time with him,

24   he shouldn't care if you show up or not. Why don't you

25   meet him after his games on Saturday?

26   LAURA: I could ask him, but I don't think he'll let me.

27   MAGGIE: Ask him?! Let you?! Is he your boyfriend or your

28   father?

29   LAURA: I don't want to hurt his feelings.

30   MAGGIE: I don't see why coming over to my house would

31   hurt his feelings. Maybe we could experiment with our

32   hair, too.

33   LAURA: Jason likes my hair this way. But I'll ask about

1   Saturday.

2   MAGGIE: What if he says no?

3   LAURA: *(Shrugs)* Then I'll go watch his softball games.

4   MAGGIE: Do you know what the date is?

5   LAURA: Sure. It's *(Use actual date, such as January 10th)*.

6   MAGGIE: I mean the year. The century. Because you talk as
7   if you are the slave and Jason is the master and you have
8   never heard of personal freedom.

9   LAURA: You don't understand. Jason's just sensitive, that's
10   all, and I want to make him happy.

11   MAGGIE: What about you? Why doesn't he want to make you
12   happy?

13   LAURA: He does make me happy.

14   MAGGIE: It doesn't sound that way to me. If he wanted you
15   to be happy, he would tell you that he'd like you to watch
16   him play softball but if you have something you'd rather
17   do, it's OK.

18   LAURA: You've never dated a college man. You don't under-
19   stand.

20   MAGGIE: I understand that you're letting Jason control your
21   life. Just because he's three years older and already in
22   college doesn't mean he should boss you around.

23   LAURA: I don't want to argue about it. Let's talk about some-
24   thing else.

25   MAGGIE: Fine. Let's talk about the pep rally. Do you have
26   any ideas for a skit?

27   LAURA: I'm not going to the pep rally.

28   MAGGIE: Why not? That's always one of the best events of
29   the year. *(Gives LAURA a suspicious look.)* Don't tell me
30   Jason won't let you.

31   LAURA: The pep rally is the same night as Jason's band
32   concert.

33   MAGGIE: And he wants you in the audience, to watch him
34   play.

35   LAURA: I want to be in the audience.

1   MAGGIE: More than you want to be in the pep rally?
2   LAURA: I just wish they weren't both at the same time.
3   MAGGIE: Remember how much fun we had at the pep rally
4   last year? Remember the baby bottle contest?
5   LAURA: *(Giggles)* And the lip synch that the seniors did?
6   MAGGIE: And Mr. Randell dressed up like a woman? *(They*
7   *both laugh.)* Are you sure you'd rather go to a band concert?
8   LAURA: I already told Jason I would.
9   MAGGIE: You know something? When you first started going
10   out with Jason, I was a little jealous. A college man seemed
11   so sophisticated. But now I feel sorry for you.
12   LAURA: That's ridiculous. I love being Jason's girlfriend.
13   MAGGIE: You're missing half the fun of high school. You can
14   never do anything with your friends anymore because you
15   always have to be Jason's shadow.
16   LAURA: I don't have to be with Jason. I choose to be.
17   MAGGIE: Why? Because you're flattered that an older guy
18   wants to go out with you?
19   LAURA: I like Jason. I think I might even love him.
20   MAGGIE: What about him? If he loves you, he sure has a
21   funny way of showing it.
22   LAURA: Jason is very nice to me.
23   MAGGIE: When you date someone, you should be friends.
24   Equals. You seem more like his pet, waiting around for a
25   pat on the head.
26   LAURA: That isn't true.
27   MAGGIE: Does he ever ask your opinion? Does he ever give
28   up his plans in order to do what you want to do? *(LAURA*
29   *turns away, looking hurt.)* Sorry. I haven't any right to
30   criticize Jason. It's just that you and I used to have such
31   good times and we don't anymore.
32   LAURA: I haven't meant to ignore you.
33   MAGGIE: I know that. And I'm glad if Jason makes you
34   happy. But will you do one thing for me? The next time
35   you have a conflict between what Jason wants you to do

1   and something else, ask yourself which one *you* really

2   want. Don't just automatically do what he wants.

3 LAURA: When you care about someone, you don't mind giving

4   up your own plans now and then in order to make that

5   person happy.

6 MAGGIE: Now and then—or the rest of your life?

7 LAURA: You know what you said about being jealous when

8   I first started going out with Jason? *(MAGGIE nods yes.)*

9   Well, I think you still are.

10 MAGGIE: *(Softly)* No. Not anymore. I'm much too fond of pep

11   rallies. *(Looks Off-stage.)* Oh. There's Andrea. I think I'll

12   see if she wants to come over Saturday. See you later. *(She*

13   *exits.)*

14 LAURA: *(Watches MAGGIE leave. Speaks wistfully.)* **To do**

15   **aerobics and make brownies.**

16

17

18

19

20

21

22

23

24

25

26

27

28

29

30

31

32

33

34

35

GOING FOR BROKE

1   *CAST:*   Two college freshmen roommates, NANCY and GLENDA.
2   NANCY is from an upper-middle-class family; GLENDA is from
3   an impoverished background.
4   *SETTING:*   The scene is their dormitory room.
5   *AT RISE:*   NANCY is packing a suitcase. GLENDA is studying.
6
7   NANCY: What time are you leaving?
8   GLENDA: I'm not going anywhere.
9   NANCY: Tomorrow is Thanksgiving. Aren't you going home?
10   GLENDA: No.
11   NANCY: *(Incredulous)* You're staying here for Thanksgiving
12   vacation?
13   GLENDA: It costs too much to go home.
14   NANCY: Well, then come home with me. Quick. Pack a bag.
15   My brother's picking me up in front of the dorm in ten
16   minutes.
17   GLENDA: I can't do that.
18   NANCY: Of course you can. My folks won't care. My brother
19   is always bringing extra people home on a holiday; my
20   parents love to have a crowd.
21   GLENDA: I have to stay here.
22   NANCY: You want to eat Dorm Glop on Thanksgiving? You're
23   out of your mind. Besides, you'll be all alone; nobody stays
24   here on Thanksgiving. Everyone goes home.
25   GLENDA: Not me. It won't be so bad. I'll get a lot of studying
26   done.
27   NANCY: We can study together at my house. First we'll stuff
28   ourselves with turkey, dressing, mashed potatoes, cran-
29   berry sauce, sweet potato casserole, Mom's homemade bis-
30   cuits, green beans, Brussels sprouts, and pumpkin pie
31   with real whipped cream, not that imitation stuff that they
32   pass off as whipped cream in the dorm dining room. And
33   then, just when you feel like you'll burst, Mom passes a

1   bowl of chocolate mints that are absolutely irresistible.
2   We'll have to diet all next week, but it will be worth it.
3   GLENDA: That isn't studying. That's an orgy.
4   NANCY: After we eat, we can crash on the living room floor
5   and study.
6   GLENDA: Sure we will.
7   NANCY: I didn't say we will. I said we could. Come on, Glenda.
8   Jason will bring us back Sunday night. There's plenty of
9   room in his car for you. And I have twin beds in my room.
10   GLENDA: I appreciate the offer, but I can't.
11   NANCY: It's unpatriotic to eat Dorm Glop on Thanksgiving.
12   No self-respecting Pilgrim would eat Macaroni Surprise.
13   GLENDA: I don't think the Pilgrims ate chocolate mints,
14   either.
15   NANCY: My brother's single. And cute.
16   GLENDA: I'd love to come. I really would. But I have to work
17   on Friday and Saturday.
18   NANCY: Tell them you're going home. Surely Jacobson's
19   Craft Store can survive for one measly weekend without
20   you.
21   GLENDA: I'm sure they could survive nicely without me. The
22   trouble is, I can't survive without them. Without their
23   paycheck, that is.
24   NANCY: You won't get fired for taking two days off. You can
25   call them from my house on Friday morning and say you're
26   sick. That won't be a lie.
27   GLENDA: Oh?
28   NANCY: You'll be sick of working while everyone else has a
29   holiday. They won't fire you for getting sick. You know
30   they won't.
31   GLENDA: *(Shakes her head no.)* I can't.
32   NANCY: Sure, you can. All you have to do is . . .
33   GLENDA: You don't understand. Even if I knew I wouldn't
34   get fired—and I don't know that at all—I *need* the pay for
35   those two days. Without it, I won't have enough for this

1   month's room and board.

2   NANCY: That's no problem. I'll lend you the money. You can

3   pay me back later.

4   GLENDA: I can't do that.

5   NANCY: Will you quit saying "I can't"? I'm telling you, grown

6   men have been known to get down on their knees and

7   plead for a piece of my mother's pumpkin pie. Oppor-

8   tunities like this only come once in a lifetime. Now, nod

9   your head up and down and repeat after me: "Yes. I can

10   do that."

11   GLENDA: I'm sorry, Nancy.

12   NANCY: Say it slowly and distinctly: "Yes. I can do that."

13   GLENDA: Thanks, anyway.

14   NANCY: Why should you miss out on one of the great

15   Thanksgiving feasts of all time, to say nothing of the plea-

16   sure of my brother's company, just because your budget

17   is a little tight this month?

18   GLENDA: My budget isn't tight this month; my budget is tight

19   this year. My budget is tight this lifetime. I can't borrow

20   money from you because I don't have any way to repay it.

21   NANCY: Why can't you repay it out of next month's salary?

22   GLENDA: I'll need next month's salary to pay next month's

23   room and board. I know it's hard for you to realize this,

24   but not everybody has the kind of money you have.

25   NANCY: I'm not exactly rich, you know. You make it sound

26   like my family is rolling in money. *(GLENDA smiles and*

27   *shrugs, but says nothing. This irritates NANCY.)* My folks

28   aren't wealthy. Believe me, I know what it's like to be poor.

29   GLENDA: *(Quietly)* No, you don't.

30   NANCY: Oh, yes, I do. Last month, I was down to only seventy-

31   five cents before my allowance check came. I couldn't even

32   buy popcorn at the movies.

33   GLENDA: How much allowance do they send you?

34   NANCY: Fifty dollars a week.

35   GLENDA: And you couldn't afford popcorn?

1   NANCY: I have to buy my own clothes out of that. It isn't all
2   fun money.
3   GLENDA: Two hundred dollars a month. I put in a lot of hours
4   at Jacobson's for two hundred dollars.
5   NANCY: When my check finally got here, I was so relieved I
6   practically cried. *(Again, GLENDA says nothing, but she rolls*
7   *her eyes and shakes her head.)* You don't believe me? You
8   think you're the only one who ever ran out of money?
9   GLENDA: No, I don't think I'm the only one. But I do know
10   that you haven't any idea of what it's like to be poor.
11   NANCY: How can you say that? You act like being poor is
12   some sort of elite club, and I can't be in it because of who
13   my parents are.
14   GLENDA: You are crazy, girl. Do you know that? You are
15   certifiably insane.
16   NANCY: That may be, but I also know what it's like not to
17   have enough money. Don't think you're the only one who's
18   ever had money problems.
19   GLENDA: Your money problems and my money problems are
20   from two different planets.
21   NANCY: No money is no money. What's so different?
22   GLENDA: You are broke until your allowance check comes.
23   I am broke until I graduate, four years from now, and get
24   a full-time job so I can support myself for the rest of my life.
25   NANCY: Don't your parents ever send you money?
26   GLENDA: No.
27   NANCY: But you get along OK with your parents. Your mom
28   writes to you.
29   GLENDA: What does that have to do with it? They *can't* send
30   money. That's the difference between being temporarily
31   broke, like you, and being poor, like me. There isn't any
32   check in the mail. There never will be.
33   NANCY: Your parents can't send you anything?
34   GLENDA: Look. Have you ever found a notice on your door
35   in the middle of winter that says your electricity is going

1   to be shut off if you don't pay the bill within twenty-four
2   hours?
3 NANCY: Well, no, but . . .
4 GLENDA: That happens to my family at least once every
5   winter. No electricity means no heat, no hot water, and
6   no lights. And it makes the landlord angry.
7 NANCY: You pay the bill, don't you? Before the power is shut
8   off?
9 GLENDA: Not always. You can't pay a bill if you don't have
10   any money.
11 NANCY: You mean your parents just let the electric company
12   turn off the power?
13 GLENDA: They don't "let" them. They have no choice.
14 NANCY: Why don't they borrow the money?
15 GLENDA: From whom? When you're poor, you don't have
16   any credit. My father can't go to a bank and ask for a loan.
17   They'd laugh him right out the door. Banks only loan
18   money to people who already have money.
19 NANCY: You could borrow from a friend or a relative.
20 GLENDA: Our friends and relatives don't have an extra hun-
21   dred dollars lying around to pay our electric bill. They're
22   all trying to scrape together enough to pay their own.
23 NANCY: How long were you without electricity?
24 GLENDA: Usually only a few days. Once it was three weeks.
25   I thought I'd never be warm again. We slept all in one bed,
26   my parents and my sister and brother and me. It was the
27   only way to keep warm enough at night.
28 NANCY: *(Softly)* That's terrible.
29 GLENDA: The trouble is, once they shut off the power, there's
30   an extra service charge to hook it back up again.
31 NANCY: How did you cook?
32 GLENDA: We ate canned beans.
33 NANCY: Cold?
34 GLENDA: Beans are good cold. Nothing wrong with cold
35   beans. When you eat them straight from the can, there

1   aren't any dishes to wash, which is a good thing when
2   there's no hot water.
3   NANCY: *(Finishes packing. Closes suitcase.)* **You're right. I don't**
4   **know what it's like. Here I am, babbling on about real**
5   **whipped cream and you . . .**
6   GLENDA: We usually had bread and peanut butter, too, from
7   the food bank. It wasn't so bad. We were poor, but we
8   were never destitute. We always had a place to sleep; we
9   managed to pay the rent. And I never had to go on a diet.
10   NANCY: I'm sorry I was so flippant about being broke.
11   GLENDA: That's OK.
12   NANCY: Look. I tell you what. Tell me how much you'll earn
13   for those two days and I'll *give* it to you. No strings attached.
14   I've got money set aside for Christmas shopping; I'll use
15   that.
16   GLENDA: Why would you want to give me that much money?
17   NANCY: Because I want you to come home with me for
18   Thanksgiving. I won't have any fun if I know you're here
19   alone, eating Dorm Glop and working at Jacobson's.
20   GLENDA: I like Dorm Glop. I like working at Jacobson's.
21   NANCY: Nobody likes Dorm Glop.
22   GLENDA: I do. I like it because I know that three times every
23   day it's going to be there. I don't care if it's Macaroni
24   Surprise again.
25   NANCY: It will be. It always is on Thursday.
26   GLENDA: It doesn't matter. What matters is not worrying if
27   there will be food on the table or not. The same with Jacob-
28   son's. I don't care if I have to stand for eight hours and
29   wait on crabby customers. I don't care if I have to work
30   when most people get a holiday. All I care is that I'm earn-
31   ing my pay. As long as I show up at Jacobson's, I will get
32   my check at the end of the week. You said when your
33   allowance check came, you almost cried from relief.
34   NANCY: That's right.
35   GLENDA: Well, let me tell you, when payday comes and I

1   hold that piece of paper in my hands, I practically cry
2   with joy. I want to shout, "Hallelujah!" because that money
3   is mine. I earned it, and no one can take it away from me.
4   It makes me proud. It makes me feel capable and indepen-
5   dent and strong, and I wouldn't trade that feeling for a
6   million turkey dinners.
7 NANCY: You know something? I envy you.
8 GLENDA: That just proves you're even crazier than I thought.
9 NANCY: When I get back from Thanksgiving vacation, I'm
10   going to look for a part-time job. I'll tell Mom and Dad
11   that I don't need an allowance anymore. It's time I earned
12   my own spending money.
13 GLENDA: You might have to eat Macaroni Surprise on Thurs-
14   days, instead of sending out for pizza like you usually do.
15 NANCY: *(With sudden realization)* **That's** why you always eat
16   Dorm Glop and never send out for pizza. Dorm Glop's free.
17 GLENDA: It isn't free. It's paid for. There's a difference.
18 NANCY: I thought maybe you didn't like pizza.
19 GLENDA: I love pizza. I don't like running out of money.
20 NANCY: Dorm Glop doesn't cost extra. Pizza does.
21 GLENDA: You're catching on.
22 NANCY: Do you think you could ask Mrs. Jacobson if she
23   plans to do any hiring?
24 GLENDA: *(Nods her head, up and down. She speaks slowly and*
25   *distinctly.)* Yes. I can do that.
26 NANCY: Thanks. *(Picks up suitcase, coat, purse.)* **Happy**
27   Thanksgiving, Glenda.
28 GLENDA: Bring back some of those chocolate mints.
29
30
31
32
33
34
35

WHOSE SIDE
IS GOD ON?

1   *CAST:*   BILL and JEFF.
2   *AT RISE:*   JEFF sits dejectedly on chair, head in hands. BILL enters.
3
4   BILL: What's wrong? Are you sick?
5   JEFF: I had an argument with Coach Nickels. At the end of
6   basketball practice, he told all of us to pray for a win
7   against Lincoln tonight.
8   BILL: Sounds like good advice. Lincoln's undefeated, you
9   know. You guys are going to need all the help you can get.
10   JEFF: Including divine intervention? Why should God care
11   who wins this basketball game?
12   BILL: Maybe it's just a figure of speech, like "keep your
13   fingers crossed." Coach Nickels wouldn't really expect you
14   to go around all day with your fingers crossed, and maybe
15   he doesn't mean you should actually pray for a win, either.
16   JEFF: He wants us to pray for a win. I hung around until
17   everyone else was gone and then I asked him. I said I'd
18   be willing to pray that we played to the best of our ability,
19   but I couldn't pray for a win.
20   BILL: What did he say?
21   JEFF: He said I could do whatever I want, but he was praying
22   for a win. I said, "What if everyone on the Lincoln squad
23   also prays to win?"
24   BILL: What are you trying to do, get bumped out of starting
25   tonight?
26   JEFF: It just bugs me that people try to use God as a means
27   to their own selfish ends.
28   BILL: It wouldn't be selfish if our team wins tonight. You'd
29   make lots of fans very happy, including me.
30   JEFF: And lots of Lincoln fans very sad.
31   BILL: I tell you what. I'll pray for you. That way, you can
32   follow your conscience and we'll still have God on our side.
33   JEFF: That's just the point. Why should God be on our side,

1   rather than Lincoln's?
2   BILL: Take it easy. I was only kidding. What got you started
3   on this, anyway? Just wanted to get in bad with the coach?
4   JEFF: I saw an interview on the news last night. It was in a
5   hospital room, and the journalist interviewed the only sur-
6   vivor of a plane crash. It was a small plane with six passen-
7   gers, and it crashed on the side of a mountain during a
8   thunderstorm. The guy was lucky he got rescued. He had
9   a broken leg, so he had to wait for someone to find him.
10   But he said something in that interview that really
11   bothered me. He said, "God was watching out for me.
12   Otherwise, I'd be dead."
13   BILL: What's wrong with that? It sounds like it was true.
14   JEFF: Didn't God care about the other people on the plane?
15   Five passengers and the pilot were killed in the crash. If
16   God was watching out for number six, why didn't he also
17   watch out for the rest of them?
18   BILL: Maybe number six is a genius. Maybe he's going to
19   invent the cure for AIDS.
20   JEFF: How do you suppose the families of those other people
21   felt if they heard that newscast? What if your parents were
22   killed in a plane crash, and the next day on TV you heard
23   the sole survivor say that he was alive because God was
24   watching out for him?
25   BILL: Are you an atheist or something?
26   JEFF: Do I have to be a genius in order to have God care
27   about me?
28   BILL: Maybe he meant God helped him after the crash, when
29   it was too late for the others.
30   JEFF: I have a hard time with that. If God would help one
31   person, I think he would help everyone. It's just like the
32   touchdown prayers.
33   BILL: The what?
34   JEFF: Somebody runs the ball in for a touchdown and then
35   he kneels down and bows his head and says a prayer,

1   **thanking God for helping him score a touchdown. Haven't**
2   **you seen them do that on TV?**
3   **BILL:**   **Yeah, I guess I have.**
4   **JEFF:**   **Why would God care who wins a football game?**
5   **BILL:**   **Maybe they aren't praying. Maybe they're just out of**
6   **breath.**
7   **JEFF:**   **You don't cross yourself when you're out of breath.**
8   **BILL:**   **What's with all this philosophy all of a sudden? Why**
9   **do you care what some guy you never met says on TV?**
10   **JEFF:**   **You're right. I guess I'm just nervous. Between the**
11   **game tonight and our big history test, my nerves are shot.**
12   **BILL:**   **Is the history test today?** *(Glances at watch)* **In less than**
13   **two minutes?**
14   **JEFF:**   **Didn't you study?**
15   **BILL:**   **I forgot all about it.** *(Closes eyes, folds hands, looks up.)*
16   **Oh, please, help me know the answers.** *(Opens eyes. JEFF*
17   *is shaking head in disgust.)* **What's the matter?**
18   **JEFF:**   **I did study. For three hours last night. So why should**
19   **God hand you the answers?**
20   **BILL:**   **Because I'm a good guy.** *(BILL exits, with JEFF following.)*
21   **JEFF:**   **Maybe I don't understand how God works.**
22
23
24
25
26
27
28
29
30
31
32
33
34
35

I KNOW I FLUNKED
THE HISTORY TEST

1   *CAST:*   Two players, KAREN and HEIDI.
2   *SETTING:*   Hallway of school.
3   *AT RISE:*   KAREN and HEIDI enter. Each carries a file folder.
4
5   **KAREN:**   **I can't look. It's too painful.**
6   **HEIDI:**   **Well, I'm looking.** *(She opens her folder and lets out a*
7   *whoop of delight.)* **I got an A! That means I'll get an A in**
8   **history for the semester.**
9   **KAREN:**   *(Glumly)* **Congratulations.**
10   **HEIDI:**   **I hoped I might. I really studied for this one.**
11   **KAREN:**   **I'll probably be grounded for the rest of the month.**
12   **HEIDI:**   **Why? What did you do?**
13   **KAREN:**   **I failed the final history test.**
14   **HEIDI:**   **How do you know? You haven't looked yet.**
15   **KAREN:**   **There's an F inside this folder. A big, red F.**
16   **HEIDI:**   **But you studied, too, didn't you?**
17   **KAREN:**   **What good would it do to study? I never get good**
18   **grades in history. There's something wrong with my**
19   **memory.**
20   **HEIDI:**   **Even if you didn't study for the test, I doubt if you**
21   **failed it. You came to class every day. You must remember**
22   **something.**
23   **KAREN:**   **I think my memory problem comes from eating too**
24   **much turkey. There's some kind of an enzyme in turkey**
25   **that makes you stupid.**
26   **HEIDI:**   **Where in the world did you hear that?**
27   **KAREN:**   **Did you ever hear of a smart turkey? They're the**
28   **most stupid creatures you can imagine.**
29   **HEIDI:**   **The Pilgrims ate a lot of turkey, and they were smart**
30   **enough to find America.**
31   **KAREN:**   **They ate the turkey after they got here.**
32   **HEIDI:**   **Forget about the turkey and look at your grade.**
33   **KAREN:**   **I never took such a hard test. All those questions**

1   about the Civil War. Who cares where battles were fought
2   so long ago?
3   HEIDI: I think it would be interesting to visit that part of the
4   country sometime. I'd like to see Gettysburg.
5   KAREN: When my folks find out I flunked the semester
6   history test, I'll be lucky if I only get grounded. They'll
7   probably disown me.
8   HEIDI: Your parents are not likely to disown their only
9   daughter.
10   KAREN: Their only stupid daughter.
11   HEIDI: And you are not likely to get an F on the test. You've
12   never had an F on any other test, have you?
13   KAREN: There's a first time for everything. Besides, Mr. Will-
14   iams hates me.
15   HEIDI: Why do you think that?
16   KAREN: He just does. I can tell by the way he squints at me.
17   HEIDI: Mr. Williams squints at everyone. I think he needs
18   glasses.
19   KAREN: It's different when he squints at me. At you, he
20   squints benevolently. At me, he squints maliciously.
21   HEIDI: You are imagining things. Mr. Williams has no reason
22   to hate you.
23   KAREN: Yes, he does. He hates me because I flunked the
24   semester test.
25   HEIDI: Let's look at your test results. Then you can worry
26   about whether Mr. Williams hates you. *(She reaches for*
27   *KAREN's folder. KAREN jerks it away.)*
28   KAREN: Of course he hates me. I am a loser. Everybody hates
29   losers.
30   HEIDI: You are not a loser.
31   KAREN: If I were a worm, all the early robins would find me.
32   HEIDI: Oh, good grief.
33   KAREN: If I were a duck, I'd be the first one in the air on
34   opening day of hunting season. *(HEIDI gives her a disgusted*
35   *look, but says nothing.)* If I were a rabbit, someone would

1   cut off my foot, to bring good luck.

2   HEIDI: Oh, gross. What is the matter with you?

3   KAREN: Nothing's the matter with me. I am simply stating

4   facts.

5   HEIDI: Well, if there was an award for negative attitude, you

6   would win it.

7   KAREN: There! You see? Even my best friend agrees that I'm

8   a loser.

9   HEIDI: Stop that. Haven't you ever heard of self-fulfilling

10   prophecy?

11   KAREN: If I have, I've forgotten.

12   HEIDI: If you believe something is going to happen, you

13   increase the chance that it will. When you think of yourself

14   as a loser, then you do things to create your own bad luck.

15   KAREN: Like flunking the most important history test of the

16   year.

17   HEIDI: You didn't expect to flunk when you took the test.

18   KAREN: Yes, I did.

19   HEIDI: If you really expected to flunk, you would not have

20   bothered to take it.

21   KAREN: I didn't know when I showed up for the test that it

22   would be so hard. Once I saw it, I expected to flunk.

23   HEIDI: Would you please open your folder and find out what

24   your grade is? *(KAREN clutches folder to her chest and shakes*

25   *her head.)* Do you want me to look for you?

26   KAREN: I don't need to look. I already know what my grade is.

27   HEIDI: How could you? Mr. Williams just handed these to us

28   three minutes ago.

29   KAREN: *(Emphatically)* I know what my grade is.

30   HEIDI: Really? *(KAREN nods yes.)* Are you telling me that you

31   really did get an F? You aren't just worrying?

32   KAREN: You know the old saying that history repeats itself?

33   Well, in my case, I'll be repeating history.

34   HEIDI: Oh. I'm sorry. Did Mr. Williams call your parents?

35   KAREN: No.

1   **HEIDI:**   **Then how did you find out?**

2   **KAREN:**   **He didn't need to call. I knew the minute I got to the**

3   **questions about the Civil War that I was doomed.**

4   **HEIDI:**   *(Losing patience)* **Have you seen your grade or haven't**

5   **you?**

6   **KAREN:**   **I don't need to see it. I told you, I already** . . . *(HEIDI*

7   *suddenly grabs KAREN's test out of her hands.)* **Hey! Give me**

8   **that.** *(HEIDI quickly opens folder and looks inside.)*

9   **HEIDI:**   **You got a C-plus.**

10   **KAREN:**   **What? No way.**

11   **HEIDI:**   **See for yourself.** *(She holds the open folder under*

12   *KAREN's nose.)* **A big, red C and a big, red plus.**

13   **KAREN:**   **Mr. Williams must have made a mistake. I think he**

14   **needs glasses.**

15   **HEIDI:**   **There's a note, too. It says, "If you would study for**

16   **these tests, you could probably get an A."**

17   **KAREN:**   **I knew it. He got my folder mixed up with someone**

18   **else's.**

19   **HEIDI:**   **All that worrying for nothing. Come on. We don't want**

20   **to be late to geometry.**

21   **KAREN:**   **It doesn't matter if I'm late or not. I'm flunking**

22   **geometry anyway.** *(HEIDI rolls eyes in disgust. They exit.)*

23

24

25

26

27

28

29

30

31

32

33

34

35

RIDING THE BIG BANANA

1   *CAST:*   Two players, GARY and BRENT.
2   *(BRENT is on scene at opening. GARY enters.)*
3
4   GARY: Happy birthday!
5   BRENT: Thanks.
6   GARY: Sixteen, at last. *(He moves his hands as if steering a car.)*
7   Driver's license, here he comes. Are you taking your
8   driver's test today?
9   BRENT: No.
10   GARY: Why not? I got my license the minute I was old enough.
11   BRENT: It won't do me any good.
12   GARY: What do you mean?
13   BRENT: I can't have a car until I'm out of high school.
14   GARY: How are you going to get to school?
15   BRENT: My parents say there is nothing wrong with riding
16   the school bus.
17   GARY: Are you kidding? They want you to keep riding The
18   Big Banana after you're old enough to drive?
19   BRENT: I told them all my friends have cars, but my parents
20   were born in the Stone Age. They think an automobile is
21   a luxury, not a necessity.
22   GARY: Get a job and buy your own car. That's what I'm doing.
23   I make just barely enough at Burger Boy to pay for the
24   car payments and insurance, but I never have to ask my
25   folks if I can use the car.
26   BRENT: They won't let me do that, either. They think a job
27   will interfere with my studies, and they like me to do extra-
28   curricular stuff.
29   GARY: Man, your parents really are prehistoric, aren't they?
30   BRENT: Most of the time, they're OK. They just don't under-
31   stand how everyone makes fun of The Big Banana. I'll
32   probably be the only senior next year who's still riding
33   the school bus. Me and all the freshmen.

1   GARY: What about your grandparents? Couldn't you wheedle
2   them into giving you a car for your birthday? If your
3   grandparents bought you a car, your parents couldn't
4   make them take it back.
5   BRENT: My grandparents are worse than Mom and Dad.
6   They say cars are the biggest air polluters of all. They
7   think it's a disgrace that kids who could ride the school
8   bus choose to drive instead.
9   GARY: That's because they never had to ride The Big Banana.
10   They don't know how embarrassing it is to line up at the
11   bus stop like kindergartners. And when it's raining, there's
12   no place dry to wait for the bus. Tell them it's a hardship.
13   Tell them you need a car so you won't get pneumonia.
14   BRENT: When they were my age, they walked four miles to
15   school. I've heard all about it a hundred times. They say
16   there was no need for fitness clubs when they were young
17   because everyone walked a lot.
18   GARY: No thanks. Why should I spend an hour walking four
19   miles when I can drive there in five minutes?
20   BRENT: It isn't so bad. I walk home quite often. When I stay
21   at school for volleyball practice or something, I'm too late
22   to ride The Big Banana so I walk home.
23   GARY: Can't you get a ride?
24   BRENT: When it's raining, I call my mom and have her pick
25   me up on her way home from work; but if it's nice weather,
26   I kind of like the walk. It gives me a chance to think.
27   GARY: I can think when I'm behind the wheel. I'd cut off my
28   arm before I'd give up my car. I mean, that car is part of
29   me. It's who I am.
30   BRENT: You're lucky.
31   GARY: I better get going, or I'll be late to work. Want to ride
32   over to Burger Boy with me and have some fries?
33   BRENT: I can't. I have volleyball practice. We have a great
34   team this year. It's really too bad you couldn't fix your
35   schedule at work so you could play.

1 GARY: Come on down after practice. I could take my break
2   and sit with you for awhile.
3 BRENT: I have to go home and bake cookies. The History
4   Club is having a potluck supper to plan a fundraiser to
5   get money for our trip. I'm supposed to bring cookies.
6 GARY: I heard about that trip. Are you guys really going to
7   go to Washington, D.C., during spring break?
8 BRENT: Yes. It's going to be great. We'll see the Lincoln
9   Memorial and the Capitol and all the other things we've
10   been learning about. I can hardly wait.
11 GARY: *(Wistfully)* I've never been to Washington, D.C.
12 BRENT: Of course, we'll have to have about a dozen car
13   washes and bake sales and other events to earn the money.
14   But those things are fun, too. We might even sponsor a
15   dance-a-thon at one of the Friday night dances.
16 GARY: I always have to work on Friday nights. Friday and
17   Saturday are the busy days at Burger Boy.
18 BRENT: But it's worth it, isn't it? I'd rather have my own car
19   than go to the Friday night dances at school.
20 GARY: At least I never have to set foot in the dreaded Big
21   Banana.
22 BRENT: You probably wouldn't like the trip to Washington,
23   D.C. We're going to take a bus tour one day.
24 GARY: Forget it. No bus tours for me. But if I have any money
25   left after I fix my carburetor, I'll come to one of your car
26   washes.
27 BRENT: Hey, that would be great.
28 GARY: See you later. My mean machine is waiting for me.
29 BRENT: *(Looks around.)* Where?
30 GARY: I had to park a couple of blocks down the street today.
31   I got here too late to get a space in the parking lot. *(He exits.)*
32 BRENT: Lucky dog. My family doesn't realize how much I'm
33   missing.
34
35

PRACTICALLY TWINS

1   *CAST:*   Two players, ELEANOR and NATASHA.

2   *(No setting necessary. Both players are On Stage at start.)*

3

4   **ELEANOR:**   This is my friend, Natasha.

5   **NATASHA:**   Who am I, really?

6   **ELEANOR:**   Natasha is a gymnast. She does the uneven paral-

7   lel bars.

8   **NATASHA:**   I enjoy gymnastics, but it is not enough to say I

9   am a gymnast. That is such a small part of me.

10   **ELEANOR:**   She gets first place in practically every gymnas-

11   tics meet. Our coach thinks she has Olympics potential.

12   **NATASHA:**   My friend, Eleanor, likes to tell people that my

13   coach thinks I have the potential to make the U.S. Olympic

14   squad someday. I wish she wouldn't always say that. I

15   want her to like me for who I am, not for how I perform

16   on the bars.

17   **ELEANOR:**   Natasha and I have been friends since third

18   grade. We live just two doors apart.

19   **NATASHA:**   Third grade. When I was in third grade I was not

20   plagued by so many unanswered questions. In the third

21   grade, I knew who I was and I knew what I wanted to do

22   with my life. I wanted to be a mail carrier. I loved to get

23   mail. I hardly ever got any, so when I did, it was a major

24   event. I thought it would be wonderful to be a mail carrier

25   and bring excitement and joy to the people on my route.

26   Later, when I learned that mail carriers bring bills and

27   advertisements, I lost my enthusiasm. The trouble is, I

28   have not replaced that enthusiasm with a new goal. What

29   do I want to be? What can I do with my life?

30   **ELEANOR:**   Imagine being good enough to make the

31   Olympics!

32   **NATASHA:**   Sometimes I get so tired of practicing my

33   routines. People don't realize how many hours of hard

1   work it takes to be good at a sport. And you have to do it
2   every day. No exceptions. But whenever I think of quitting,
3   I can't. If I quit, I'd never know whether I would have
4   made it or not.
5 ELEANOR: Natasha's parents are both doctors. No wonder
6   she's so smart. No wonder she never gets sick. I'm always
7   getting a cold or the chicken pox or a touch of the flu, but
8   Natasha is strong as an elephant.
9 NATASHA: People are too impressed with doctors. The min-
10   ute anyone finds out that my parents are doctors they
11   make three assumptions: 1. We are rich; 2. My parents are
12   brilliant; 3. I will be a doctor someday, too.
13 ELEANOR: I suppose Natasha will go to medical school even-
14   tually, but I hope she trains for the Olympics first.
15 NATASHA: I have no desire to be a doctor. For most families,
16   dinner table conversation is about sports or current events
17   or what happened in school. My family discusses the com-
18   plications of gallbladder surgery or so-and-so's white
19   blood count or patient X's liver disease. It isn't very appe-
20   tizing, let me tell you.
21 ELEANOR: Except for her parents being doctors and her
22   being so good at gymnastics, Natasha and I are pretty
23   much the same. We even go to the same church.
24 NATASHA: Eleanor likes church; she believes what they say.
25   I question everything. My parents say I have to go until
26   I'm sixteen because they want me to have some kind of
27   religious background. They say I can decide for myself
28   then.
29 ELEANOR: I feel so blessed to have a friend like Natasha. I
30   hope that we'll always be this close.
31 NATASHA: When I'm sixteen, I'll quit going. Or I'll try other
32   churches.
33 ELEANOR: We go to the same school and have the same
34   friends. We're practically twins.
35 NATASHA: Eleanor has a whole circle of friends. I'm included

1 in all their activities, but they aren't really my friends.
2 They are acquaintances. I like all the kids in our group,
3 but I never think the way they do. I always feel different,
4 like I don't quite fit in.
5 ELEANOR: If Natasha ever moved away, I think I'd die of
6 loneliness. I tell her everything—and she tells me every-
7 thing, too. The amazing thing is, we always agree. We think
8 exactly alike.
9 NATASHA: It's lonely to feel different. Eleanor's lucky. She'll
10 go through life happy, doing what's expected of her, never
11 challenging the rules. It must feel comfortable to just accept
12 things as they are and never hunger for more.
13 ELEANOR: Natasha's lucky. It must be wonderful to be smart
14 and talented. I'm ordinary; my life is predictable. I'll prob-
15 ably get a clerical job after high school and get married
16 a couple of years later and raise a family. Not that there's
17 anything wrong with any of that, but it means I may live
18 my whole life right here, within shouting distance of where
19 I started kindergarten.
20 NATASHA: When I think of all the options, it's scary. I want
21 to see other countries, learn other languages, experience
22 other thinking. I want to stretch my mind.
23 ELEANOR: There won't ever be any extraordinary excite-
24 ment in my life. My thrills will have to come vicariously,
25 through knowing people like Natasha.
26 NATASHA: Life was easier when all I wanted was to deliver
27 the mail.
28 ELEANOR: I wish I could be on an Olympic team.
29
30
31
32
33
34
35

A NORMAL
FATHER-SON CONVERSATION

1   *CAST:*   Two male players, DAD and SON.

2   *SETTING:*   Scene is interior of home. This can be sketchy; the only

3   necessary props are a small TV and a telephone.

4   *AT RISE:*   DAD is seated, intently watching a baseball game on

5   TV. *(Back of TV is toward audience.)* SON enters.

6

7   SON: Can I talk to you, Dad?

8   DAD: Just a minute. The Giants have the bases loaded.

9   SON: It's important.

10   DAD: *(Sighs. Clicks off TV.)* What is it that's so important it

11   can't wait until the end of the inning?

12   SON: Nothing. Go ahead and watch the ball game. A baseball

13   game is more important than your son.

14   DAD: I turned it off, didn't I?

15   SON: Only because I insisted.

16   DAD: Do you want to tell me something or not?

17   SON: Forget it.

18   DAD: I turned off the Giants in the bottom of the ninth with

19   the bases loaded and the score tied at one-all, just so you

20   could tell me to forget it? What's the matter with you?

21   SON: Nothing's the matter with me. Nothing that a normal

22   father-son conversation couldn't fix.

23   DAD: I am normal. I am ready to converse.

24   SON: It isn't the same when I have to beg for your attention.

25   If you don't want to talk to me of your own free will, then

26   it isn't any good.

27   DAD: You were the one who wanted to talk.

28   SON: I was. I am.

29   DAD: So, talk.

30   SON: Uh, how's work, Dad?

31   DAD: What?

32   SON: Work. You know, that office you go to for ten hours

33   every Monday through Friday. How's everything there?

1   **DAD: OK. No problems. Work is OK.** *(Slight pause)* **How's**
2   **school?**
3   **SON: OK. No problems there, either. School's OK.**
4   **DAD: Good. Well, now that we have that out of the way, is it**
5   **all right if I see how the game turned out?** *(He reaches toward*
6   *TV.)*
7   **SON:**   *(Blurts this, quickly.)* **When you met Mom, how did you**
8   **know she was the right girl for you?**
9   **DAD:**   *(Sits back, without touching knob.)* **I didn't. I took a chance.**
10   **SON: It wasn't love at first sight?**
11   **DAD: Do you think you're in love? Is that what this is all about?**
12   **SON: Me? Are you kidding? Who would I be in love with?**
13   **DAD: I don't know. Lisa Ellensworth, maybe?**
14   **SON: Lisa? No way.**
15   **DAD: She's cute.**
16   **SON: Do you think so?**
17   **DAD: Don't you?**
18   **SON: Well, sure, but I didn't think anyone else had noticed.**
19   **DAD: When a girl looks the way Lisa looks, people notice.**
20   **SON: I suppose so.**
21   **DAD: Have you asked her to go out with you?**
22   **SON: She'd never go out with me.**
23   **DAD: Why not? There's nothing wrong with you. You come**
24   **from a good family.**
25   **SON: She's a brain.**
26   **DAD: You're no idiot.**
27   **SON: I don't know how to ask a girl to go out.**
28   **DAD: Call her on the telephone.**
29   **SON: I don't know what to say.**
30   **DAD: When she answers, say, "Lisa, this is Mark. Would you**
31   **like to go to a movie with me next Saturday?"**
32   **SON: What if she says no?**
33   **DAD: Then you say, "How about some other time?"**
34   **SON: What if she's saying no because she would never go out**
35   **with me under any circumstances?**

1   DAD: You'll be able to tell if she's saying no because she can't
2   go that night or no because she wouldn't go out with you
3   for a million dollars.
4   SON: How? How can I tell?
5   DAD: You'll just know it. Trust me.
6   SON: Maybe I'll wait until tomorrow and ask her in person.
7   DAD: It's easier on the phone. Especially if she says no.
8   SON: You think she's going to say no, don't you? You're right.
9   Why would a gorgeous, smart girl like Lisa want to go out
10   with me?
11 DAD: Because you're a handsome, smart boy. What's her
12   number?
13 SON: 747-0382.
14 DAD: *(He picks up telephone and hands it to SON.)* Dial it. Right
15   now, before you get cold feet.
16 SON: I already have cold feet.
17 DAD: If you don't call her, ten minutes from now you'll wish
18   you had.
19 SON: You're right. I'll do it. *(He punches the numbers quickly,*
20   *filled with determination.)*
21 DAD: Good. And I'm going to watch the end of the ball game.
22   *(He turns TV on.)*
23 SON: Hello, Lisa? This is Mark. Would you like to go to the
24   movie with me on Saturday? You would? Are you sure? I
25   mean, that's great. I'll see you at school tomorrow, and
26   we can decide what time. Yes. 'Bye. *(DAD leans closer to*
27   *TV, trying to hear. He looks excited and shakes one fist in the air.)*
28 SON: She said yes.
29 DAD: Good.
30 SON: I can't believe it. Lisa Ellensworth is going out with me
31   Saturday night.
32 DAD: Look at this. It's the top of the eleventh, and the Giants
33   have runners on first and second with no outs.
34 SON: The biggest event of my life has just transpired. How
35   can you care about a baseball game?

1   **DAD:**   **Oh, no. Not a double play. Rats!**

2   **SON:**   *(Shouts.)* **Dad!**

3   **DAD:**   *(Looks away from TV, at SON.)* **What? What is it?**

4   **SON:**   **Thanks, Dad.**

5   **DAD:**   **You're welcome.** *(SON just stands there, grinning.)* **Would**

6   **you like to watch the ball game with me?**

7   **SON:**   **No. I have to get ready.**

8   **DAD:**   **For what?**

9   **SON:**   **For my date with Lisa.**

10   **DAD:**   **I thought you were going on Saturday.**

11   **SON:**   **I am. We are.**

12   **DAD:**   **Well, if you need to get ready, don't let me keep you.**

13   **SON:**   *(Exiting)* **I can't believe she said yes. Lisa said yes.**

14   **DAD:**   **A strike? He called that a strike! That ball was inside**

15   **by a mile.**

16

17

18

19

20

21

22

23

24

25

26

27

28

29

30

31

32

33

34

35

PROM NIGHT PARTY

1   *CAST:*   Two female players, KELLY and JOAN.
2   *SETTING:*   Optional.
3

4   **KELLY:**   Are you nervous about Saturday night?
5   **JOAN:**   No. I'm excited, but I'm not nervous.
6   **KELLY:**   Well, I'm scared to death.
7   **JOAN:**   Why? You've gone out with Tim lots of times.
8   **KELLY:**   Not to the prom.
9   **JOAN:**   The prom won't be that much different than other
10   dates, except we'll be more dressed up and we'll get home
11   later.
12   **KELLY:**   If you and Glen weren't double-dating with Tim and
13   me, I'd probably chicken out.
14   **JOAN:**   That's the silliest thing I ever heard. You sound like
15   you're afraid to go to your own high school prom.
16   **KELLY:**   It isn't the prom part that scares me. It's—you know.
17   Afterwards.
18   **JOAN:**   The party? You've been to a hundred parties.
19   **KELLY:**   Not in a hotel suite. Not where the guys rent extra
20   rooms to use privately.
21   **JOAN:**   What are you talking about? What extra rooms?
22   **KELLY:**   You don't know about the rooms?
23   **JOAN:**   No.
24   **KELLY:**   They do it every year. The guys rent a couple of extra
25   rooms and then one couple at a time leaves the party and
26   goes off by themselves to—well, you know. Every couple
27   takes a turn, and when they come back, everyone else
28   cheers.
29   **JOAN:**   Are you saying that every couple who attends the
30   party at The Cheshire Suites is planning to—to use one of
31   those rooms? *(KELLY nods yes.)* You and Tim? *(KELLY nods*
32   *yes again.)* You're planning to—to have sex that night?
33   **KELLY:**   That's what I'm nervous about.

1   JOAN: Oh. Do you think Glen is expecting *me* to—to use one
2   of those rooms with him?
3   KELLY: Sure. Everyone does it. Every year, during the after-
4   prom party, everyone . . .
5   JOAN: I don't believe you. My sister went to the prom last
6   year and she didn't. At least, I don't think she did. She
7   never said anything about it.
8   KELLY: I doubt she would have come home and made a fam-
9   ily announcement.
10   JOAN: Well, I'm not doing it. Not prom night. Not with Glen.
11   KELLY: I thought you liked Glen.
12   JOAN: I do like him. But we've only gone out one other time.
13   I barely know him.
14   KELLY: You were so excited when he asked you to go with
15   him.
16   JOAN: I thought he was only asking me to go to the prom. I
17   didn't know he was inviting me to go to bed, too.
18   KELLY: What are you going to do?
19   JOAN: What do you mean?
20   KELLY: Are you going to tell Glen ahead of time?
21   JOAN: You want me to tell him that I have no intention of
22   having sex with him, when the subject has never come up?
23   KELLY: You can't wait until prom night and then tell him no.
24   JOAN: He might be relieved. Maybe Glen doesn't want to use
25   one of those private rooms any more than I do.
26   KELLY: Ha! *All* the guys want to. Tim can hardly wait.
27   JOAN: He said that? You've discussed this?
28   KELLY: The subject has come up. What's wrong with that?
29   JOAN: It seems so—so calculated. Like making an appoint-
30   ment. "Let me check my calendar. Yes, I'm available on
31   Saturday at two a.m. to lose my virginity. I'll write it
32   down."
33   KELLY: That isn't funny.
34   JOAN: Are you sure you want to keep that appointment?
35   KELLY: There has to be a first time.

1   JOAN: You didn't answer my question.
2   KELLY: No. I'm not sure. But Tim is sure, and he thinks I am,
3   too. We've joked about it. He showed me the condoms he
4   bought. We've come close a couple of times before.
5   JOAN: Don't let Tim decide what you want. You can always
6   stick with me that night. I'm not leaving the group.
7   KELLY: What if Glen gets mad and takes you home early?
8   JOAN: Then I'll know he's not the kind of person I want to
9   go out with again. But I don't think he'd be angry if I
10   refuse to go to bed with him on our second date.
11 KELLY: Tim would get mad.
12 JOAN: Maybe not. He might be disappointed, especially if
13   you've talked about it and let him think you feel the same
14   way he does about it. I think *you're* the one who should
15   say something ahead of time.
16 KELLY: Are you kidding? And take a chance of breaking up,
17   two days before the prom?
18 JOAN: If Tim would break up with you over this, he isn't
19   someone you want to be so serious with.
20 KELLY: I'm not missing out on my senior prom.
21 JOAN: Maybe you're wrong when you say everyone uses
22   those rooms. How do you know that?
23 KELLY: Tim told me.
24 JOAN: Are you sure he isn't stretching the truth a little? May-
25   be one group of kids did that; it doesn't mean everyone
26   did. And it certainly doesn't mean you have to.
27 KELLY: I can't accuse Tim of lying to me.
28 JOAN: Do you want Tim to be honest with you about his
29   feelings?
30 KELLY: Well, sure.
31 JOAN: Then be honest with him.
32 KELLY: That's easy for you to say.
33 JOAN: How would you feel if Tim told you he doesn't want
34   to go to the hotel party after the prom?
35 KELLY: Ecstatic.

1   JOAN: Now you're scared to death. If Tim said no, you'd be
2   ecstatic. That ought to tell you something.
3   KELLY: When I was in junior high, I thought the senior prom
4   would be a carefree, wonderful, fun night. How did it get
5   so complicated?
6   JOAN: I plan to have a carefree, wonderful, fun time on Satur-
7   day. Without a private room.
8
9
10
11
12
13
14
15
16
17
18
19
20
21
22
23
24
25
26
27
28
29
30
31
32
33
34
35

I'LL BE THERE

1   *CAST:*   Two male players, KEN and SAM.
2   *(No special setting required. KEN and SAM are On Stage at*
3   *start.)*
4
5   **KEN:**   Are you going to go to the school play tonight?
6   **SAM:**   No. There's good TV on. It's part three of a show that
7   I saw the first two parts of.
8   **KEN:**   Can't you tape it and watch it later?
9   **SAM:**   I suppose I could, but I'm tired and I'll have to rush
10   like crazy to get to the play on time. It just doesn't sound
11   like much fun.
12   **KEN:**   Ginny and Ron will be disappointed if you don't go.
13   They're hoping for a sell-out.
14   **SAM:**   I know.
15   **KEN:**   Once you get there, you'll like it. And you can sleep late
16   tomorrow, can't you?
17   **SAM:**   No. It's my aunt and uncle's wedding anniversary, and
18   we have to go to a family reunion. My parents want to
19   leave early to have time to visit with all the relatives. I
20   tried to talk them into letting me stay home, but they
21   wouldn't buy it. They said when people want to celebrate
22   the fact that they have been married for twenty-five years,
23   the least their relatives can do is be there to celebrate with
24   them. Or, as my mom put it, "I'd rather spend a day this
25   way than to listen to them crying over a divorce." But I
26   still wish I didn't have to go.
27   **KEN:**   Maybe you can sleep in the car.
28   **SAM:**   Maybe.
29   **KEN:**   I'm going to try to get there early tonight, so I can sit
30   down in front. If you decide to come, I could save you a seat.
31   **SAM:**   No, thanks. I'm going to skip the play.
32   **KEN:**   Remember when I had that violin solo in the winter
33   concert and I was so nervous and excited?

1	SAM: I heard you did great. I was sorry I couldn't get there
2	to hear it.
3	KEN: I was sorry, too. Ginny and Ron came. Neither of them
4	love orchestra music, but they came because they're my
5	friends. When there was an event that was important to
6	me, they showed up. They went to my baseball game, too,
7	the first time I was the starting pitcher. They cheered so
8	loud it was embarrassing, but it helped me relax and I
9	pitched a good game.
10	SAM: I can see why you feel obligated to go to the play.
11	KEN: I'm not sure obligated is the right word. It will be fun
12	to go to the play. It seems to me that when you care about
13	someone, then you show up for the important events in
14	their life.
15	SAM: There'll be tons of people at the play tonight. It won't
16	matter if I go or not. They probably won't even miss me.
17	KEN: They may not miss you, but if you go and then stay
18	around afterwards to tell them what you liked about it, I
19	guarantee they'll notice. They'll appreciate it.
20	SAM: Friends understand if you don't want to do something.
21	Ginny and Ron would say just because they wanted to be
22	in a play doesn't mean that everyone they know has to
23	come to see it.
24	KEN: They go to all your football games.
25	SAM: That's different. Everybody goes to the football games.
26	Well, I better get going. Tell Ginny and Ron I'm sorry I
27	couldn't make it to their play.
28	KEN: Are you?
29	SAM: What's that supposed to mean?
30	KEN: You want me to lie and tell them you're sorry you can't
31	come when the truth is, you could go if you wanted to.
32	SAM: I don't see why you're making such a big deal out of
33	the school play. It isn't as if Ginny and Ron were opening
34	on Broadway.
35	KEN: When you're flaked out in front of the TV tonight, will

1   you do one thing for me?

2   SAM: What?

3   KEN: Think how you would like it if you had a birthday party

4   and nobody came. Or it was the first football game of the

5   season and all of the fans decided to stay home and watch

6   television. Or you graduated and your whole family had

7   other plans that day and didn't come to your graduation.

8   SAM: Forget it. None of that would ever happen. You're just

9   trying to make me feel guilty because I'd rather stay home

10   and watch my program than come back to school and

11   watch the play. Well, I'm sorry, but the play just isn't that

12   important to me.

13   KEN: The play isn't important to me, either.

14   SAM: Then why are you going?

15   KEN: Because Ginny and Ron are.

16

17

18

19

20

21

22

23

24

25

26

27

28

29

30

31

32

33

34

35

HUMAN BEANS

1 *CAST:* Two female players, MARY and PAULA.
2 *AT RISE:* PAULA is On Stage at start. MARY enters, walks toward
3   PAULA as she speaks.
4
5 MARY: Are you ready for the great biology experiment?
6 PAULA: No.
7 MARY: Me either. Cutting up a dead frog is not exactly my
8   idea of a good time.
9 PAULA: That's for sure.
10 MARY: Well, let's go get it over with.
11 PAULA: Go ahead. I'll see you later.
12 MARY: What about you?
13 PAULA: I'm not going.
14 MARY: Why not? Are you sick?
15 PAULA: No. I'm just not going to biology today.
16 MARY: You're cutting class?
17 PAULA: I'm going to go sit in the library.
18 MARY: You can't! This class is required. You'll get an incom-
19   plete for the semester.
20 PAULA: I know. I've decided to take the incomplete rather
21   than dissect the frog.
22 MARY: It won't be that bad. My sister did it last year, and
23   she said except for the smell it wasn't as awful as everyone
24   says it is. If my sister can do it without getting sick, you'll
25   be able to do it.
26 PAULA: I don't *want* to do it. I think it's wrong. Why should
27   all those frogs be killed, just so we can cut them open? I
28   am capable of learning about the inside of a frog in other
29   ways. I don't need personal experience.
30 MARY: It's only a frog, Paula. It isn't like we were going to
31   cut up somebody's pet poodle.
32 PAULA: Would it be wrong to kill a pet poodle and dissect it
33   in class?

1   MARY: Are you kidding? Of course it would be wrong!

2   PAULA: Why is that any worse than killing the frogs?

3   MARY: It just is.

4   PAULA: I'm not sure the frogs would agree.

5   MARY: Do you think the frogs have rights? Is that it?

6   PAULA: The frogs have a right to live.

7   MARY: The frogs aren't living. They're already dead. They
8   won't know they're being dissected.

9   PAULA: I'll know. If I go to class today, I'll be saying I think
10   it was OK to kill all those frogs.

11   MARY: Geez, Paula. You make it sound like we were going
12   to line the frogs up and strangle them. *(PAULA shrugs and*
13   *says nothing.)* I'm not going to kill any frog. That part's
14   already done.

15   PAULA: The frogs are dead, all the same.

16   MARY: This isn't murder, you know. It's a scientific experi-
17   ment.

18   PAULA: There are other ways to learn. Better ways.

19   MARY: You sound like you care more about animals than
20   people.

21   PAULA: I care about both.

22   MARY: If you get an incomplete in biology, you'll wreck your
23   grade-point average. You might not be able to play vol-
24   leyball next year.

25   PAULA: I know.

26   MARY: You're willing to give up volleyball because of a stupid
27   frog?

28   PAULA: No. But I'm willing to give up volleyball in order to
29   stand up for what I believe.

30   MARY: I think you're making a big mistake.

31   PAULA: I've thought about this a lot. I've decided that when
32   you think something is wrong and you do it anyway, you
33   have compromised. You're a lesser person from then on.

34   MARY: What about the rest of the volleyball team? Isn't it
35   wrong to let them down? We have a good chance of win-

1   ning the district tournament next year, if you're playing.

2   Come on Paula. The frog isn't worth such a sacrifice.

3   PAULA: I think it is.

4   MARY: You might be giving up a sports scholarship. A pro

5   career!

6   PAULA: Not likely.

7   MARY: A million-dollar contract!

8   PAULA: Don't forget the cereal commercials.

9   MARY: OK, OK. So maybe you won't make it as a professional

10   volleyball player.

11   PAULA: I don't *want* to be a professional volleyball player.

12   MARY: Mr. Mackett will probably ask me where you are.

13   What do you want me to tell him?

14   PAULA: He won't ask. He already knows I'm not coming. I

15   went in yesterday after school and asked if I could do an

16   alternate assignment, instead of taking the incomplete.

17   MARY: He said no?

18   PAULA: He said if he let me do an alternate assignment other

19   kids would want to do one, too.

20   MARY: He's right about that. Given a choice, I'd take the

21   alternate assignment. Most people would.

22   PAULA: Most people don't want to dissect a frog—and yet,

23   everyone is going to do it anyway.

24   MARY: No one wants an incomplete in a major subject. You'll

25   probably have to go to summer school to make it up.

26   PAULA: If everyone who takes biology refused to dissect a

27   frog, what do you think would happen?

28   MARY: I don't know. Mr. Mackett can't give an incomplete

29   to the entire tenth grade.

30   PAULA: If everybody cut class today and refused to partici-

31   pate, maybe next year's classes would not be required to

32   dissect frogs.

33   MARY: And there would be no extracurricular sports at all.

34   They're only frogs, They aren't human beings.

35   PAULA: When I was a little kid, my big brother used to tease

1   me by calling me a human being. I thought he said human
2   bean, b-e-a-n, and I pictured a long, skinny, green person.
3   I used to cry and shout that I wasn't a bean. I was in third
4   grade before I figured out that he was saying human being.
5 MARY: What does that have to do with biology class?
6 PAULA: A couple of years ago, a funny thing happened. I
7   decided I don't want to be a human being *(enunciate clearly:*
8   *being)* either.
9 MARY: You want to be a frog?
10 PAULA: Instead of a human being, I want to be a human
11   doing. I don't want simply to be—to wait until something
12   happens and then react to it. That's too passive. I want to
13   take action.
14 MARY: Couldn't you take some action that would still let you
15   play volleyball next year? You're the best spiker this
16   school has had in a long time.
17 PAULA: Thanks.
18 MARY: People will say you're a wimp, that you're staying
19   away because you're squeamish.
20 PAULA: I wrote an article for the school paper, explaining
21   how I feel. It will be in the next issue.
22 MARY: Do your parents know you're doing this?
23 PAULA: Yes. They said it's my decision.
24 MARY: If I got an incomplete, my parents would have a fit.
25   I'd be grounded for a month.
26 PAULA: I'm not asking you to cut class with me.
27 MARY: Then I guess I'll be going. *(She starts to leave, hesitates,*
28   *turns back to PAULA.)* Are you *sure* you want to do this?
29 PAULA: I'm sure.
30 MARY: But you're the only one. It won't make any difference.
31   Nothing will change. Next year's biology students will still
32   be cutting up frogs.
33 PAULA: It will make a difference. It'll make a few people
34   question whether I'm right or wrong. When they talk about
35   me and about whether I'll get to play volleyball, they'll

1   also think about compassion and cruelty. They'll wonder,
2   maybe for the first time, whether it is right for humans to
3   use other species as laboratory tools.
4   MARY: You know something? I think you're crazy, but I ad-
5   mire your guts for standing up for what you think.
6   PAULA: Thanks.
7   MARY: Well, here I go. Mr. Frog is waiting. *(She hurries almost*
8   *to exit, then stops.)* Before I saw you, I was only worried
9   about getting sick in class. Now I feel kind of sorry for
10   the frog. *(She exits.)*
11   PAULA: And I feel sorry for the human beings who will dis-
12   sect them. *(She exits, the opposite way from Mary.)*
13
14
15
16
17
18
19
20
21
22
23
24
25
26
27
28
29
30
31
32
33
34
35

THE UGLIEST HAIR
IN THE WORLD

1 *CAST:* Two females, RUTH and CHAR.
2 *SETTING:* Optional.
3
4 RUTH: Look at my hair. Have you ever seen such ugly hair?
5 No, wait. Don't answer. I don't want to hear it.
6 CHAR: What's wrong with your hair?
7 RUTH: What's wrong with my hair? Are you serious?
8 CHAR: It looks OK to me.
9 RUTH: Run. Do not walk, run to your nearest eye doctor and
10 make an appointment. You may be going blind.
11 CHAR: There's nothing wrong with my eyes, and there's noth-
12 ing wrong with your hair, either.
13 RUTH: For your information, I have the ugliest hair in the
14 world.
15 CHAR: That isn't true. I've seen lots uglier hair.
16 RUTH: Where? In the zoo?
17 CHAR: You can get a comb through your hair. Mine is like
18 combing a bird's nest.
19 RUTH: Have you noticed how sexy the women in shampoo
20 commercials are? They barely move and their silky, long
21 hair swirls around their shoulders.
22 CHAR: They do it with off-camera fans. Your hair would swirl
23 sexily, too, if a couple of high-powered fans were blowing
24 air at you.
25 RUTH: My hair would not swirl sexily if I was caught in a
26 hurricane.
27 CHAR: If you were caught in a hurricane, you wouldn't care
28 what your hair did.
29 RUTH: I'm going to shave my head.
30 CHAR: Oh, great. Why don't you have your nose pierced while
31 you're at it?
32 RUTH: If I shaved my head, I would never again have to
33 worry about my hair.

1　CHAR:　You think being bald will make you sexy?
2　RUTH:　I have tried every combination of shampoo, condition-
3　　　　ers, and highlighters known to womankind and my hair
4　　　　remains exactly the same, dull shade of mouse.
5　CHAR:　You're too hard on yourself. I like your hair. At least
6　　　　you have some natural curl. How would you like to be
7　　　　stuck with my hair—straight as a yardstick and just about
8　　　　as exciting?
9　RUTH:　I would trade hair with you any day. Yours is thick
10　　　　and shiny. Mine is so thin I could probably shave it off
11　　　　with one stroke of the razor.
12　CHAR:　Well, don't try. I guarantee that if you shave your
13　　　　head, you will regret it. Do you have any idea of how
14　　　　people would stare?
15　RUTH:　At least they'd notice me. I'd rather be stared at than
16　　　　ignored.
17　CHAR:　Maybe you should get a perm. Your hair might have
18　　　　more body if it was permed.
19　RUTH:　I got a perm two weeks ago.
20　CHAR:　Oh. I hadn't noticed.
21　RUTH:　Nobody noticed. That's my point exactly. Since my
22　　　　hair is the same as invisible, why don't I just get rid of it?
23　CHAR:　I'm sorry I didn't notice your perm. It doesn't seem
24　　　　any curlier. Are you sure they left the solution on long
25　　　　enough?
26　RUTH:　It was plenty curly the first day. It was so frizzed I
27　　　　had it straightened.
28　CHAR:　No wonder I didn't notice. You undid it before I saw
29　　　　you.
30　RUTH:　It cost me a total of sixty-five dollars, and I ended up
31　　　　looking exactly the way I started.
32　CHAR:　I was thinking of getting a perm, but you've changed
33　　　　my mind.
34　RUTH:　Why would you want a perm?
35　CHAR:　Because I hate my hair the way it is.

1   RUTH: You are insane. Why would you hate your hair? Your
2   hair is gorgeous.
3   CHAR: All the ends are split. I look like I should be riding a
4   broom.
5   RUTH: There must be something wrong with your mirror.
6   You are not describing the person I am talking to.
7   CHAR: It's also too long.
8   RUTH: So try wearing it short. Maybe you'd like it better
9   short.
10   CHAR: I used to wear it short. It took me three years to grow
11   it out to this length, and now I hate it.
12   RUTH: If you hate it long, why don't you get it cut?
13   CHAR: I hated it short, too. When it was short, I always
14   thought if I could only wait until my hair grew out, I would
15   love it. Instead, I have the ugliest hair in the world.
16   RUTH: I already said that. *I* have the ugliest hair in the world.
17   CHAR: Then I have the ugliest hair in the universe.
18   RUTH: We could both dye our hair. Maybe if we were red-
19   heads, we would be happy.
20   CHAR: I doubt it. I don't really want red hair.
21   RUTH: Neither do I.
22   CHAR: Let's forget about our hair. We're stuck with it, so let's
23   just forget it.
24   RUTH: Good plan. I will not mention my hair again.
25   CHAR: Neither will I.
26   RUTH: Now if I could only do something about my nose.
27   CHAR: *Your* nose? Don't you mean *my* nose?
28
29
30
31
32
33
34
35

PAST INJUSTICES

1   *CAST:*   Two brothers, HARRY and MIKE.
2   *(Scene can be anything: Two chairs or a complete room or simply*
3   *a bare stage. HARRY and MIKE are On Stage at start.)*
4
5   **HARRY:**   My friend Ronnie got a cat today. A little black kitten.
6   **MIKE:**   That's nice.
7   **HARRY:**   His parents didn't know he was going to get it, but
8   they let him keep it anyway.
9   **MIKE:**   Now don't start in about that.
10   **HARRY:**   His sister got it for him. Somebody had a box of free
11   kittens outside the grocery store, and Ronnie's sister took
12   one. Without asking her parents. Do you know what they
13   said when they found out?
14   **MIKE:**   Look. The cat business was ten years ago. Forget it.
15   **HARRY:**   They said, "It's OK with us if you want a cat."
16   **MIKE:**   Good. That was very nice of them.
17   **HARRY:**   I couldn't believe it. Ronnie's parents came home
18   from work, and there were Ronnie and his sister on the
19   floor, playing with a kitten, and all they said was that it
20   was OK with them.
21   **MIKE:**   Lucky Ronnie.
22   **HARRY:**   Nobody yelled. Nobody had six fits. And nobody
23   grabbed the innocent little kitten and took it off to death
24   row.
25   **MIKE:**   You don't know for sure that Felix died. Maybe he got
26   adopted.
27   **HARRY:**   And maybe I won the lottery.
28   **MIKE:**   If you did, will you lend me ten dollars?
29   **HARRY:**   I didn't win the lottery, dodo brain. And Felix didn't
30   get adopted. He got a lethal injection in his furry little . . .
31   **MIKE:**   Stop it! I don't want to hear this again.
32   **HARRY:**   You don't want to face the fact that our parents
33   deliberately took our kitten away from us and sentenced

1   it to death.
2 MIKE: Maybe. Maybe Felix died, and maybe he didn't.
3 HARRY: You saw the stats. More than seventy percent of the
4   cats taken to the shelter were euthanized.
5 MIKE: And almost thirty percent were adopted.
6 HARRY: The point is, Mom and Dad took the chance. Even
7   with odds like that, they left Felix at the shelter.
8 MIKE: Don't get so worked up. It was ten years ago. Felix
9   would probably be dead by now anyway.
10 HARRY: So would Abraham Lincoln. Does that mean John
11   Wilkes Booth did the right thing?
12 MIKE: Let's talk about something else.
13 HARRY: When I saw Ronnie with that cat, I wanted to cry. I
14   felt like I was four years old again.
15 MIKE: Well, you aren't. You should forgive Mom and Dad for
16   the Felix business and then forget about it.
17 HARRY: Forget about it? How can I forget something like
18   that?
19 MIKE: For starters, we could quit talking about it.
20 HARRY: I cried myself to sleep every night for almost a year.
21   What they did was a form of child abuse. I won't ever
22   forget it. I'll never forgive them, either, and frankly, I
23   don't understand how you can dismiss it so easily. Do you
24   like to see little animals suffer?
25 MIKE: Felix didn't suffer. Even if he was euthanized, it was
26   done humanely.
27 HARRY: Well, I suffered. I'm in pain every time I think about it.
28 MIKE: Then quit thinking about it. Let it go. You can't change
29   the past, so why keep replaying it?
30 HARRY: Mom and Dad have never understood how I feel.
31   Sometimes I think the hospital made a mistake and gave
32   me to the wrong parents when I was born.
33 MIKE: I agree. My real brother would never keep whining
34   about something that happened ten years ago.
35 HARRY: It isn't just Felix. It's everything. It's my whole life.

1   They don't understand anything about me. They have no
2   idea who I am.
3 MIKE: They probably assume you are Harry Ryan Tupman,
4   since that's what they named you.
5 HARRY: Inside. They don't understand what I care about,
6   what's important to me. They don't know who I am inside.
7 MIKE: So, who are you?
8 HARRY: You don't understand, either.
9 MIKE: Maybe not. But here's what I think. I think you've got
10   some problems right now. You got a low grade on your
11   math test, or you had a fight with Jennifer, or Coach
12   chewed you out at practice or something. Something went
13   wrong and you're frustrated and unhappy, and then your
14   friend got a cat so you blame Mom and Dad for everything
15   that's wrong in your life.
16 HARRY: What are you, my personal shrink?
17 MIKE: You've always blamed Mom and Dad for everything
18   that goes wrong.
19 HARRY: It's usually their fault.
20 MIKE: Wrong, bucko. Your problems are not Mom and Dad's
21   fault. Having a kitten when you were four years old would
22   not have helped you get an A in math or make the starting
23   squad in basketball.
24 HARRY: You're simplifying it too much. It isn't just the kitten.
25 MIKE: There are a lot of kids with really rotten parents or
26   no parents at all. You could have done much worse than
27   Mom and Dad. At least they tried.
28 HARRY: *(False enthusiasm)* Hooray! Felix is dead! Long live
29   his killers.
30 MIKE: I don't know why I bother talking to you.
31 HARRY: You know what's wrong with you? You have no
32   sense of injustice. Someone can deliberately trample on
33   your feelings, and you don't even care.
34 MIKE: Mom and Dad are not perfect. I'll grant you that. But
35   they took us places when we were little. They played cards

1   with us and read us stories. They bought us toys. They
2   *tried*, which is more than a lot of parents do. They made mis-
3   takes, but they never deliberately trampled on our feelings.
4   HARRY: How could anyone take a defenseless little kitten to
5   the animal shelter?
6   MIKE: In a few years, you'll be on your own and you can
7   have as many cats as you want. You can go down to the
8   animal shelter and adopt every stray kitten in the place.
9   HARRY: That won't bring Felix back.
10   MIKE: Neither will complaining about something that can't
11   be changed.
12   HARRY: Ronnie got a cat now, not in a few years.
13   MIKE: Then visit him if you need to see a cat. Or call up the
14   SPCA or one of the other animal protection agencies and
15   ask if they need a volunteer. You could help all the other
16   Felixes of the world. Do something constructive for a
17   change, instead of moaning about how your life is ruined
18   because Mom and Dad wouldn't let you keep a stray cat
19   that you brought home when you were four years old.
20   HARRY: Remember when we had to change schools? When
21   we couldn't go to John Quincy Adams School anymore?
22   MIKE: How could I *not* remember, with you here to remind me?
23   HARRY: Remember that? Is that an example of parents who
24   care about their kids? I only had one good friend in the
25   third grade. One friend! Jackson Smith. The one person I
26   really cared about and who cared about me, and Mom
27   and Dad made me leave him and go to a different school.
28   MIKE: Mom and Dad didn't make you go to a different school.
29   The school board did. It wasn't Mom and Dad's fault that
30   the district changed the boundaries and that we happened
31   to live in an area that switched schools.
32   HARRY: They should have refused to transfer me. They
33   should have picketed the school board.
34   MIKE: They went to the meetings. They said they preferred
35   to have us stay at John Quincy Adams, and the school

1   board said no. What did you want them to do—lie down
2   in front of the school bus and refuse to move?
3   HARRY: My whole life would be different if I'd been allowed
4   to stay at John Quincy Adams School.
5   MIKE: Now that is completely ridiculous. I had to change
6   schools, too, you know. When you were in third grade, I
7   was in second grade. I had to leave John Quincy and trans-
8   fer to Elm Grove. I had to leave my friends, just the same
9   as you. I didn't like it any better than you did.
10 HARRY: You didn't have Jackson Smith for a best friend.
11 MIKE: I made new friends. You moped around and told
12   everyone within earshot that John Quincy Adams was a
13   better school than Elm Grove.
14 HARRY: It was.
15 MIKE: The kids at Elm Grove didn't think so.
16 HARRY: I never had another friend that I liked as much as
17   Jackson.
18 MIKE: How come you didn't stay in touch with him?
19 HARRY: When you're in the third grade and suddenly you
20   don't see someone every day like you used to, you lose
21   contact.
22 MIKE: We have a telephone. Even in the third grade you knew
23   how to use it. Did you ever call him?
24 HARRY: What good would it have done? Mom and Dad . . .
25 MIKE: Call him now.
26 HARRY: Are you crazy? I haven't seen him since third grade.
27 MIKE: So? Call him up and say you got to thinking about how
28   much fun you used to have in third grade and you were
29   just wondering how he's doing. Maybe you could get
30   together.
31 HARRY: I can't call Jackson after all these years.
32 MIKE: You can if you want to. You aren't helpless. If you
33   don't like your situation, look for a solution. Quit blaming
34   everyone else for your problems.
35 HARRY: I wish Mom and Dad were like Ronnie's parents.

1 MIKE: And I wish I had naturally curly hair.
2 HARRY: That's another thing! Remember when I decided to
3   let my hair grow long and Mom made me get it cut? Re-
4   member that? It was in sixth grade, and she dragged me
5   to the barber and he butched me, and I wore a paper bag
6   on my head so no one would see my short hair. Do you
7   remember that haircut?
8 MIKE: I don't remember the haircut. I do remember being
9   embarrassed because my big brother was walking around
10   with a paper bag over his face. Come to think of it, that's
11   probably why I only got a C-plus on my English theme
12   today. I couldn't do enough in-depth research because of
13   the latent inhibitions brought on by acute embarrassment
14   over my brother's behavior when he was in the sixth grade.
15 HARRY: That is the most ridiculous statement anyone has
16   ever made. What does my behavior in sixth grade have to
17   do with how well you write an English theme now?
18 MIKE: I rest my case.
19
20
21
22
23
24
25
26
27
28
29
30
31
32
33
34
35

WILL I KILL YOU,
IF I HAVE TO?

1   *CAST:*   Two players, TED and NAOKO.
2   *AT RISE:*   TED and NAOKO stand a few feet apart, facing each
3   other.
4
5   TED: I don't know you. Never met you. For me, you have no
6   identity and no face. I know you by only one name: Enemy.
7   NAOKO: You. *You* are the enemy.
8   TED: My country and your country do not agree on anything
9   except the fact that we must go to war with each other.
10 NAOKO: *(He turns to face audience.)* It is my duty to serve in
11   the war. I must fulfill my duty.
12 TED: *(He turns to face audience.)* I love my country. Always
13   have. I love to hear "The Star Spangled Banner" before
14   the ball game. I mean, where else but in the good old U.S.
15   of A. can you have a hot dog at the ball park and watch
16   the San Diego Chicken do tricks?
17 NAOKO: My people have lived many hundreds of years on
18   this land. My father was a farmer and his father before
19   him. I will be a farmer, too, when the war is over.
20 TED: That's what I'll miss the most, in the war. Sports. But
21   it'll be worth it. When I finish my time in the Army, I'll go
22   to college and Uncle Sam will pay the bill.
23 NAOKO: I hope our land survives the war. Bombs and mines;
24   they destroy land for many years. Nothing grows.
25 TED: That Sally ticks me off. I go over to tell her the big news
26   that I've enlisted, and instead of getting excited, she starts
27   to cry. "Killing is wrong," she says, "no matter what cause
28   you're defending."
29 NAOKO: Farming is good. Farmers see growth and renewal.
30   There is no growth and renewal in war.
31 TED: So I asked her how Hitler would have been stopped if
32   no one had been willing to stand up and fight. Her only
33   answer was, "You can't create peace by declaring war."

1   NAOKO: I am frightened. I wear the uniform, but I am not a
2   soldier in my heart. In my heart, I am always a farmer.
3   TED: The land of the free and the home of the brave. "I am
4   one of the brave," I told her, "and I'm proud to defend my
5   country."
6   NAOKO: I hope I will not disgrace my family by acting
7   cowardly.
8   TED: "They're people, too," she said. "They have families who
9   love them. They hurt and bleed and die, the same as we
10   do." Now, what kind of remark is that? I mean, I don't
11   *want* to kill anybody. I'm no maniac murderer. I'm just
12   willing to defend my country. That's all. Just doing a job
13   that has to be done. I thought she'd be proud of me. Instead,
14   she acts like it's a crime.
15   NAOKO: My mother weeps—my father turns away. They can-
16   not bear to say goodbye, for they have seen war before.
17   TED: Maybe when I get back, there'll be a parade, with bands
18   and flags, and everybody cheering. Then Sally will know
19   what a hero is. Then she'll quit yakking about being a
20   citizen of the world, instead of a citizen of the United
21   States. I never heard of a parade for someone who calls
22   themselves a citizen of the world.
23   NAOKO: I know there are farmers in America, too. Do they
24   labor over their crops in dry years as we do? Do they
25   struggle to save a sick animal?
26   TED: It'll be fast. I'll be back before I know it. We have bigger
27   guns and faster planes and better technology.
28   NAOKO: How odd that we farmers should point guns at each
29   other, when we are so much alike.
30   TED: They won't know what hit them.
31   NAOKO: Why can't our leaders resolve their differences? Why
32   can't we find a peaceful solution?
33   *(During next speech, TED and NAOKO slowly turn to face each*
34   *other again.)*
35   TED: I wonder if I'll ever actually have to kill someone. I mean,

1   I know I can do it if I have to, but I hope it won't be up
2   close. Dropping a bomb is one thing. Pointing a gun at
3   somebody's head . . . *(TED shakes his head, as if to get rid of*
4   *such thoughts.)* Geez, I'm getting as bad as Sally. I won't be
5   pointing a gun at anybody except the enemy, so why
6   should I worry?
7 NAOKO: You. You are the enemy.

BASEBALL FANATIC

1 **CAST:** Two players, AL and GUS.
2 **SETTING:** GUS's home. GUS is On Stage at start.
3   *(AL enters.)*
4

5 AL: What are you doing? Do you want to do something
6   together?
7 GUS: I'm going to watch the baseball game. You can watch
8   it with me, if you want to.
9 AL: No, thanks. I thought we might rent a video or go get
10   some peppermint chocolate chip ice cream.
11 GUS: Not me. I wouldn't leave now if the house was burning.
12 AL: I don't see what you're so excited about. It's only a
13   baseball game.
14 GUS: Wrong. It is game five of the World Series.
15 AL: So? Neither of the teams is from around here. Why do
16   you care who wins?
17 GUS: I don't care who wins.
18 AL: Then why watch?
19 GUS: Because it's a chance to see good baseball. Maybe even
20   some *great* baseball. A triple play. A no-hitter. A grand
21   slam.
22 AL: Think of all you could do in the three hours you're going
23   to sit in front of the tube.
24 GUS: Like watch a video and eat ice cream?
25 AL: You could accomplish something.
26 GUS: I'll accomplish something tomorrow. Tonight, I'm
27   watching the baseball game.
28 AL: By this time next year, you won't even remember who
29   was playing.
30 GUS: Don't bet on it. My mother watched a no-hitter once,
31   before she was married, and she still talks about that game.
32   It's one of her most exciting memories.
33 AL: Your mother must lead a pretty dull life.

1 GUS: Not really. She has three kids, owns a small business,
2   and is a volunteer for the Red Cross. She always has about
3   six things going on at once.
4 AL: Oh.
5 GUS: But she still loves baseball.
6 AL: I suppose it relaxes her. Like a soap opera.
7 GUS: You've never watched a ball game with my mother or
8   you wouldn't say it relaxes her. She can out-yell any three
9   normal fans.
10 AL: Maybe that's why you're a baseball fanatic. It's in your
11   genes.
12 GUS: I'm not a fanatic. I just happen to enjoy a sport.
13 AL: You wouldn't leave the game if the house was burning,
14   but you aren't a fanatic.
15 GUS: Don't you have a hobby? What do you do in your spare
16   time?
17 AL: I paint.
18 GUS: Good. You paint; I watch baseball.
19 AL: Painting uses my hands. And my mind.
20 GUS: I use my hands and my mind; I keep score.
21 AL: Writing down two numbers at the end of the game does
22   not count as using your hands.
23 GUS: I score the whole game. You know, write down what
24   every batter does each inning.
25 AL: Why would you want to do that?
26 GUS: Because it's interesting. That way, when player X comes
27   up to bat in the sixth, I can look at my score card and
28   know exactly what he did in his previous at-bats.
29 AL: You mean, if somebody strikes out, you write down,
30   "struck out"?
31 GUS: No. If they strike out, I write "K." That's the symbol for
32   strike out.
33 AL: You use a secret code?
34 GUS: It's no secret. Everyone knows that "K" means "strike
35   out."

1 AL: I didn't.
2 GUS: Baseball fans know.
3 AL: It sounds childish. Kids love secret codes.
4 GUS: Kids like to paint, too.
5 AL: Painting has a tangible end result.
6 GUS: So does baseball.
7 AL: What? What do you have to show for your time after you
8   watch a ball game?
9 GUS: Satisfaction. Three hours from now, I will be a happy
10   person. Especially if I see a no-hitter or a great play.
11 AL: I suppose there's no use trying to change you.
12 GUS: That's right.
13 AL: If your own mother sets a bad example, you're probably
14   a hopeless case.
15 GUS: I happen to think my mother set a good example. She
16   taught me to have fun. To relax. She taught me that a
17   well-balanced person takes time to enjoy life. Human bat-
18   teries need to be recharged now and then. You do it by
19   painting; I do it by watching the World Series.
20 AL: And you don't feel guilty?
21 GUS: For what? Why should I feel guilty?
22 AL: For wasting your time.
23 GUS: I'm not wasting time.
24 AL: I can see there's no point talking to you.
25 GUS: Good. The game's going to start, and I don't want to
26   miss anything. *(AL shakes head in disgust and exits.)* **Play**
27   **ball!**
28
29
30
31
32
33
34
35

NEW WAYS
TO SAY NO

1   *CAST:*   Two players, EILEEN and MERNA.

2   *SETTING:*   No special setting required. EILEEN and MERNA are

3   On Stage at start.

4

5   EILEEN: I got in trouble again. No TV for a month.

6   MERNA: What did you do this time?

7   EILEEN: I got home late. My curfew was 10 o'clock, and I

8   didn't get there until 11:30. My mother was ready to call

9   the hospitals, to see if I'd been admitted.

10   MERNA: What happened? Why were you so late?

11   EILEEN: I went to the library with Kay and we met some

12   friends of hers there, and they asked us to go out for pizza

13   with them. I really didn't want to—I knew I'd be late if I

14   went—but I could tell Kay wanted to go with them and I

15   hated to be a party pooper.

16   MERNA: The last time you got grounded it was because you

17   used your mother's charge card for that dress that you

18   said you really didn't want, but the clerk talked you into

19   buying.

20   EILEEN: The one my mother made me return.

21   MERNA: You could save yourself a lot of grief if you learned

22   how to say no. Especially when it's something you don't

23   want to do in the first place.

24   EILEEN: Easier said than done.

25   MERNA: Not if you practice. Tell you what. I will give you

26   some lessons right now. New Ways to Say No. You may

27   take notes if you wish so that you can practice when you're

28   by yourself.

29   EILEEN: You're nuts.

30   MERNA: Maybe so, but I've found I get along a lot better since

31   I've learned to say no to things that I don't want to do. Or

32   would you rather continue to get grounded all the time?

33   EILEEN: All right. What do I have to do?

1 MERNA: Lesson number one: This is for cases like last night,
2   when someone is pressuring you to go somewhere and
3   you know you should go home instead. This is what you
4   say: "I'm sorry; I can't go. It really sounds like fun, but
5   my mother worries herself sick when I get home late. You
6   guys go on without me."
7 EILEEN: What if they keep arguing? What if they pressure me?
8 MERNA: Then you repeat, "I'm sorry; I can't go." Try it.
9 EILEEN: I'm sorry; I can't go.
10 MERNA: Again.
11 EILEEN: I'm sorry; I can't go.
12 MERNA: That wasn't so hard, was it?
13 EILEEN: Not with you. You aren't trying to get me to go any-
14   where.
15 MERNA: Lesson number two: This is for the times when you
16   blurt out yes and then instantly wish you hadn't.
17 EILEEN: That's me. I do that all the time.
18 MERNA: The next time you do it, say: "I made a mistake. I
19   should not have said yes, and I'll have to back out."
20 EILEEN: You have to be kidding. I could never say that.
21 MERNA: Sure you can. Practice it right now. Just say, "I
22   made a mistake. I should not have said yes, and I have to
23   back out."
24 EILEEN: I made a mistake. I should not have said yes, and I
25   have to back out.
26 MERNA: Good! You're getting the hang of it. Lesson number
27   three is for the times when you realize it's important for
28   your own safety to say no, like when someone who has
29   been drinking offers to drive you home or when somebody
30   wants you to take drugs. You say: "I don't want to do that."
31   Period. No reasons, no explanations, no arguments. Just
32   say, "I don't want to do that."
33 EILEEN: I don't want to do that.
34 MERNA: If they keep insisting, or call you chicken, repeat
35   the same thing: "I don't want to do that." Eventually, they'll

1	give up and find someone else to hassle.
2	EILEEN: I don't want to do that.
3	MERNA: You got it. Lesson number four is easy. It's for when
4	someone calls you and wants you to do something and
5	you don't want to do it, even though you aren't doing any-
6	thing else.
7	EILEEN: Yes! Like the other night. I had just made a big bowl
8	of popcorn and was going to watch my favorite movie when
9	Carrie called and wanted me to go ride bikes with her.
10	MERNA: What did you do?
11	EILEEN: I went. But it wasn't any fun. I just wasn't in the
12	mood for riding my bike.
13	MERNA: Next time, say this: "Thanks for asking, but I've been
14	super busy lately and I need a night by myself, just to be
15	lazy."
16	EILEEN: She'd be insulted. That's like saying I would rather
17	watch my movie alone than go bike riding with her.
18	MERNA: Wouldn't you?
19	EILEEN: Not always. But that night, yes, I wanted to watch
20	my movie. Alone.
21	MERNA: Then you should have told her that. She wouldn't
22	be offended. Everyone has times when they need to be
23	alone. Say, "Thanks for asking, but I've been super busy
24	lately and I need a night by myself, just to be lazy."
25	EILEEN: You make it sound so easy.
26	MERNA: It is easy, once you make up your mind. And after
27	you say no, you'll have this incredible feeling of relief that
28	you don't have to do something you don't want to do.
29	EILEEN: That would be a pleasant change. Usually, I feel
30	resentful because I am doing something I don't want to do.
31	MERNA: Practice at home. Say the "no" phrases over and
32	over until they come easily for you.
33	EILEEN: OK. I'll try it.
34	MERNA: Good luck.
35	EILEEN: Thanks. And thanks for your help.

1   MERNA: No problem. *(She starts to exit.)* I'll see you at seven
2   on Saturday.
3   EILEEN: Seven?
4   MERNA: The river run, remember? Everyone is going to meet
5   at seven Saturday morning and run the five miles along
6   the river bank to the county park and then have a picnic
7   breakfast.
8   EILEEN: I didn't know it was going to be so early. I have to
9   babysit Friday night. I thought the river run was in the
10   afternoon.
11   MERNA: Nope. It's seven in the morning. We want to run
12   before it gets hot. See you there.
13   EILEEN: No.
14   MERNA: What?
15   EILEEN: I made a mistake. I should not have said yes, and
16   I'll have to back out.
17   MERNA: You don't want to do the river run?
18   EILEEN: Not so early in the morning when I have to babysit
19   late the night before. *(They look at each other for one beat.*
20   *Then MERNA smiles.)*
21   MERNA: OK.
22   EILEEN: You aren't mad?
23   MERNA: How can I be mad? I'm the one who told you to say
24   no. *(Both exit.)*
25
26
27
28
29
30
31
32
33
34
35

36

FLOWERS WON'T
BRING BILLY BACK

1   *CAST:*   Two players, HELEN and ANNE.

2   *SETTING:*   Optional.

3   *(ANNE is On Stage when scene opens. HELEN rushes in.)*

4

5   HELEN: Have you heard the news?

6   ANNE: What news?

7   HELEN: About Margie's little brother?

8   ANNE: What about him? What happened?

9   HELEN: He died.

10   ANNE: Died! Are you sure?

11   HELEN: Mrs. Winthrop called my mom about an hour ago.

12   When Margie's mother went to get Billy up this morning,

13   she found him dead in his crib.

14   ANNE: Oh, that's terrible. I didn't even know he was sick.

15   HELEN: He wasn't. It was Sudden Infant Death Syndrome.

16   It happens sometimes; for no reason at all, a perfectly

17   healthy baby just quits breathing.

18   ANNE: Poor Margie. She was so excited when Billy was born.

19   What are we going to do? How can we help?

20   HELEN: There's nothing anyone can do. He's already dead.

21   ANNE: I mean, what are we going to do for Margie?

22   HELEN: I guess we could send her a sympathy card.

23   ANNE: I think we should buy some flowers and go over to

24   her house.

25   HELEN: Flowers won't bring Billy back.

26   ANNE: Maybe Margie wants someone to talk to.

27   HELEN: We'd be in the way. They probably don't want visi-

28   tors now.

29   ANNE: We could just give our flowers to whoever answers

30   the door and ask them to tell Margie we're there if she

31   wants to see us but if she doesn't, we'll understand.

32   HELEN: Flowers wilt.

33   ANNE: We could collect money from everyone at school and

1   contribute it for research about Sudden Infant Death Syn-
2   drome.
3 HELEN: Everyone I know is broke. Including me. We couldn't
4   collect enough to make a difference in the research.
5 ANNE: But Margie and her family would know we tried to
6   help.
7 HELEN: Have you ever tried to collect money for a charity?
8   It takes forever. People say they want to contribute, but
9   no one ever remembers to bring the money.
10 ANNE: Margie's parents must be devastated. She told me that
11   they had wanted another baby ever since Margie was three
12   years old.
13 HELEN: He was a cute little guy, too. Always grinning and
14   drooling.
15 ANNE: I know! Let's bake muffins and take them over. No-
16   body in their family is going to feel like cooking, but sooner
17   or later they'll get hungry.
18 HELEN: What if Margie thinks we're just snoopy? You know,
19   like we want to come over and watch her cry.
20 ANNE: I don't want to watch Margie cry. I just want her to
21   know that I feel bad, too. I wouldn't want her to think that
22   nobody except her family cares that Billy died.
23 HELEN: It's just so awkward. I'm afraid I'll say the wrong
24   thing.
25 ANNE: All I plan to say is, "I'm sorry."
26 HELEN: Still, it isn't the same as if an old person dies. You
27   expect somebody's grandfather to die, but not their baby
28   brother.
29 ANNE: All the more reason we should let Margie know that
30   we're thinking about her.
31 HELEN: Let's go tell Julie the news. She's going to be so
32   shocked. She even baby-sat with Billy a couple of times
33   when Margie's folks came to watch Margie play in the
34   volleyball games at school.
35 ANNE: You go ahead. I think I'll make those muffins and take

1   them over for Margie's family.
2   HELEN: What if they don't want to talk to you?
3   ANNE: Then I'll leave the muffins and come home.
4   HELEN: What if they get mad?
5   ANNE: They'll know I came out of love and concern. They'll
6   understand that I want to show sympathy. How is Margie
7   going to know how we feel if we don't tell her?
8   HELEN: Well, good luck. I'm going to go find Julie. *(She starts*
9   *toward exit.)* This is the worst tragedy that's ever happened
10   to anyone I know. *(She exits.)*
11   ANNE: I wonder if Margie likes blueberry muffins or banana
12   muffins. Maybe I'll make some of each.
13
14
15
16
17
18
19
20
21
22
23
24
25
26
27
28
29
30
31
32
33
34
35

37

FRIENDS FOREVER

1   *CAST:*   Two players, CINDY and DONNA.

2   *AT RISE:*   CINDY and DONNA stand apart. Their words are di-

3   rected to the audience, not to each other.

4

5   CINDY: We vowed we'd be friends forever. We said we'd al-

6   ways sit together at lunch and call each other every night

7   and always tell each other everything.

8   DONNA: I feel bad about Cindy. I know I've hurt her feelings,

9   and I don't know what to do about it.

10   CINDY: I never thought Donna would be like this. We used

11   to have such fun. We used to be so close.

12   DONNA: She wants everything to stay just the same as it al-

13   ways was. Including me. But I can't stay the same. I've

14   changed.

15   CINDY: We used to spend every Saturday together. We'd

16   wash our hair and try out different styles. We'd browse

17   through all the shops at the mall. We'd talk for hours.

18   Donna never wants to spend time alone with me anymore.

19   Every Saturday, she's busy with that dumb conservation

20   group of hers.

21   DONNA: I invited Cindy to come with me one Saturday, but

22   she said no. To tell the truth, I was relieved. She doesn't

23   fit in with my new friends. It sounds snobbish to say this,

24   but I don't know any other way to put it: I've outgrown

25   Cindy. She still thinks the way we did when we were nine

26   years old.

27   CINDY: I'm all for a clean environment and saving the earth

28   and all of that, but my idea of fun is not volunteering at

29   a recycle center. Who wants to work with all that trash?

30   DONNA: We don't have anything in common anymore. Cindy

31   wants to talk about earrings and which cute boy said what

32   and whether she should wear her blue sweater or her

33   green one. The same things she talked about last week

1   and last year.

2   CINDY: Donna gets all worked up about politics and civil
3   rights and conservation. If you ask me, all that's a waste
4   of energy. One person can't change anything.

5   DONNA: Don't get me wrong. I like pretty clothes and boys,
6   but they are not the focus of my life. I want to help improve
7   our society. I want to make a difference.

8   CINDY: I suppose I should just forget about Donna and find
9   someone else to hang out with. But it's hard to forget her.
10   She was always so funny and bright. I always felt more
11   alive when I was with her.

12   DONNA: A friend should accept you just the way you are, with-
13   out wanting to change you. It's hard to do. If I accept Cindy
14   as she is, I don't enjoy spending time with her. I keep
15   wishing she would grow, mentally. I wouldn't even care
16   if she disagreed with my opinions; at least we could have
17   an interesting discussion. As it is now, she doesn't have
18   any opinion about anything that matters. She's stagnant.

19   CINDY: The last time Donna and I ate lunch together, she
20   acted bored. It's been months since we talked on the tele-
21   phone for more than a few minutes. When I called her,
22   she said she couldn't talk because she had to practice her
23   speech. She ran for student body president and won.

24   DONNA: There is so much I want to do. Sometimes I feel like
25   a volcano, bubbling and overflowing with ideas and plans
26   and energy.

27   CINDY: I voted for her. She'll be a good president. There is
28   so much she wants to accomplish. I'm not like that, and I
29   never will be. I feel bad to lose Donna as my best friend.
30   I'll probably never have another friend like her.

31   DONNA: I promised Cindy we'd be friends forever. At the
32   time, I truly believed we would be. She'll always be special
33   to me. I'll always care what happens to her. But I have to
34   move on, without her.

35   CINDY: People should keep their promises.

38

STICKS AND STONES

1   *CAST:*   Two players, MEGAN and SANDI.
2   *SETTING:*   At school.
3
4   MEGAN: Oh, no. I got Mr. Carlson for English.
5   SANDI: What's wrong with Mr. Carlson? My sister had him
6   last year, and she liked him.
7   MEGAN: He's a fag. Oh, great. I'll be spending an hour five
8   times a week with a fag. *(SANDI turns away, offended, but*
9   *says nothing.)* What's the matter? Didn't you know he's a
10   fag? I thought everyone in the whole school knew that.
11   SANDI: Unless Mr. Carlson has posted a sign, I don't see how
12   everyone in school could know his personal business. And
13   even if he is gay, I don't think you should call him a fag.
14   It's derogatory.
15   MEGAN: Well, don't get huffy. It's only a name.
16   SANDI: You had Mrs. Richards for math this year, didn't you?
17   MEGAN: Yes. I really liked her.
18   SANDI: Did you ever call her a nigger?
19   MEGAN: *(Shocked)* No! Of course not. What a terrible thing to
20   say.
21   SANDI: I don't think it's any worse than calling Mr. Carlson
22   a fag.
23   MEGAN: It isn't the same thing at all. Nigger is a horrible
24   racial slur, and I'm surprised you would use it. How do
25   you think Mrs. Richards would feel if she heard you?
26   SANDI: How do you think Mr. Carlson would feel if he heard
27   you call him a fag?
28   MEGAN: Mrs. Richards can't help what color skin she was
29   born with.
30   SANDI: And Mr. Carlson can't help what sexual preference
31   he was born with.
32   MEGAN: Why are you defending him?
33   SANDI: Because I get tired of hearing kids make jokes about

1   gay people when they don't know anything about it.
2   MEGAN: And you do?
3   SANDI: As a matter of fact, yes, I do. My parents have some
4   friends, Bill and Ken, who are gay. They're nice people.
5   They're smart and kind and lots of fun.
6   MEGAN: And perverted.
7   SANDI: No! They've been together for almost twenty years.
8   They own a house, and they have a little dog, and when
9   you go to their home, you get a feeling that—that love
10   exists there.
11   MEGAN: Oh, man! I never thought I'd hear someone like you
12   talking about a couple of queers being in love.
13   SANDI: I've known Bill and Ken ever since I was a little kid.
14   I always liked to see them when they came over for dinner
15   because they didn't ignore me, like some of my parents'
16   friends did. They always talked to me and *listened*, and
17   sometimes they would bring me a little gift. It wasn't until
18   last year that I began to suspect that Bill and Ken are a
19   gay couple. I hinted around to my mother, and she told
20   me, yes, they are.
21   MEGAN: I cannot imagine my parents inviting anyone like
22   that to our house.
23   SANDI: Why not?
24   MEGAN: They might—you know, go after my little brother.
25   SANDI: There would be absolutely no chance of that.
26   MEGAN: How do you know?
27   SANDI: Because I know these people, and they are not child
28   molesters.
29   MEGAN: I saw part of a Gay Rights parade on the news one
30   night. Those people are disgusting.
31   SANDI: I saw that, too. I agree; they were too radical. But
32   I've seen peace demonstrators get offensive, too. Also ani-
33   mal rights activitists and people on both sides of the abor-
34   tion issue and lots of others. Just because some gays were
35   loud and rude doesn't mean they all act that way. It's like

1   judging all teenagers by the way gangs behave.
2   MEGAN: I don't see why you're defending them. *You* aren't
3   gay, are you?
4   SANDI: No, I'm not.
5   MEGAN: I didn't think so, but people will start to think you
6   are if you aren't careful how you talk.
7   SANDI: That's exactly what this conversation is all about—
8   being careful how you talk.
9   MEGAN: I don't see why you're so touchy.
10   SANDI: Do you remember that movie we saw, about the
11   Japanese Americans who were put in camps during World
12   War II?
13   MEGAN: Yes. Talk about unfair!
14   SANDI: My grandma says she knew a Japanese family, and
15   she can remember people calling them "dirty yellow Japs"
16   and saying how terrible they were. The family she knew
17   were all decent people and loyal citizens, and she realized
18   it was unfair to blame them for something they hadn't
19   done. But she never spoke up. Grandma says it's one of
20   the few things she regrets in life—that she lacked the cour-
21   age to defend her friends.
22   MEGAN: I don't see what your grandma has to do with Mr.
23   Carlson.
24   SANDI: I'm trying not to repeat her mistake. Bill and Ken are
25   my friends.
26   MEGAN: Do they carry purses?
27   SANDI: That is a stereotype. Bill and Ken look exactly like
28   any of my parents' other friends. They dress the same.
29   They talk the same.
30   MEGAN: What do they do? What kind of work?
31   SANDI: Bill's a hospital administrator, and Ken sells life in-
32   surance. They collect antique music boxes. They take their
33   collection to nursing homes and put on programs for the
34   patients. They're good people.
35   MEGAN: Well, I'm glad they're *your* friends and not mine.

1   SANDI: I'm glad they're my friends, too. That's why it
2   bothered me to hear you insult Mr. Carlson. He's a good
3   teacher. Whether he's gay or not, he doesn't deserve to be
4   called "fag."
5   MEGAN: It's only a name. You know the old saying, "Sticks
6   and stones may break my bones, but names can never
7   hurt me."
8   SANDI: Not all old sayings are true.
9   MEGAN: Well, I still wish I had somebody else for English.
10
11
12
13
14
15
16
17
18
19
20
21
22
23
24
25
26
27
28
29
30
31
32
33
34
35

39

ALL I WANT FOR CHRISTMAS
IS TO NOT BE PREGNANT

1   *CAST:*   Two players, DENISE and STACY.
2   `   (As scene opens, DENISE and STACY are seated together.)
3
4   DENISE: Thanks for coming over.
5   STACY: What happened? What's so important?
6   DENISE: I'm pregnant.
7   STACY: Are you positive?
8   DENISE: I got one of those little kits at the drug store, where
9   you can test yourself.
10   STACY: Have you told Brian?
11   DENISE: Not yet.
12   STACY: What about your parents?
13   DENISE: Are you kidding? I haven't told anybody, except you.
14   STACY: When are you going to tell them?
15   DENISE: Never.
16   STACY: Sooner or later, they'll find out.
17   DENISE: Maybe not. Not if I have an abortion.
18   STACY: Is that what you want to do?
19   DENISE: No. But I don't want to have a baby, either.
20   STACY: What other options are there?
21   DENISE: I could kill myself.
22   STACY: Oh, Denise. Don't say that. You're too bright. You
23   have too much to live for.
24   DENISE: If I'm so bright, how come I'm pregnant?
25   STACY: Everybody makes mistakes.
26   DENISE: I really didn't think it would happen to me. *(Slams*
27   *fist into other palm.)* Why weren't we more careful? I know
28   about birth control. Why didn't we use it?
29   STACY: There's no point questioning what's already done.
30   DENISE: I'm scared.
31   STACY: I don't blame you. But I'll help you. So will your
32   parents; I'm sure of it.
33   DENISE: I can't tell them. Just thinking about it makes me

1   want to throw up.

2 STACY: You probably want to throw up because you're preg-
3   nant.

4 DENISE: And Grandma. Who's going to tell Grandma? She's
5   coming for Christmas, and now I'm going to spoil her
6   whole visit.

7 STACY: If you killed yourself, it would spoil her whole life.
8   To say nothing of what it would do to your parents.

9 DENISE: I won't kill myself.

10 STACY: Promise?

11 DENISE: Promise.

12 STACY: Good.

13 DENISE: Maybe I'll get hit by a cement truck.

14 STACY: The first thing you need to do is tell Brian. And then
15   your folks. Let them help you decide what to do.

16 DENISE: I won't get married. Even if Brian says he wants to
17   marry me, I won't do it like this. For the rest of my life,
18   I'd know the only reason he married me was because I
19   was pregnant.

20 STACY: He'd think the same thing—that the only reason you
21   married him was because you were pregnant.

22 DENISE: Maybe I won't tell him.

23 STACY: This is his problem, too. You didn't get pregnant
24   alone, you know.

25 DENISE: It may be his problem, but it's my body. Eight
26   months from now, he isn't going to look any different.

27 STACY: I think you should go to the doctor. Be positive that
28   you are pregnant before you tell anyone.

29 DENISE: I'm afraid Dr. Winston will tell my folks. He's known
30   them for years. He plays golf with Dad.

31 STACY: Then go to someone you don't know. Go to Planned
32   Parenthood.

33 DENISE: Have you ever had a pelvic exam?

34 STACY: No.

35 DENISE: Neither have I. It sounds awful.

1   STACY: It can't be too bad. Millions of women have them
2   every year.
3   DENISE: When I decided to have sex with Brian, I thought I
4   was so sophisticated. Every time we did it, I felt smug and
5   grown-up. It was my big secret from the world.
6   STACY: You could talk to one of the counselors at school.
7   DENISE: What would you do, if you were me? Would you
8   have an abortion?
9   STACY: I don't know what I would do. Even if I did, my deci-
10   sion wouldn't necessarily be the right one for you.
11   DENISE: What if I had an abortion and then later, years from
12   now when I'm grown up and ready to have a baby, I can't
13   get pregnant? My parents know these people who have
14   been trying for ten years to have a baby. They've spent
15   thousands of dollars on fertility clinics, and she still isn't
16   pregnant. What if that happens to me?
17   STACY: You can't worry about every faint possibility. You
18   got pregnant easily this time . . .
19   DENISE: Too easily.
20   STACY: Chances are you could do it again.
21   DENISE: Do you hate me?
22   STACY: Of course not. No one else is going to hate you, either.
23   DENISE: Grandma is.
24   STACY: She might be shocked at first, but she won't hate you.
25   DENISE: Shocked. And disappointed. I've let everybody
26   down.
27   STACY: If you want me to be here when you tell your folks,
28   let me know and I'll come over.
29   DENISE: If I have a girl, I'll name her Stacy.
30   STACY: Just don't name the baby Stacy if it's a boy.
31   DENISE: I don't want to have an abortion. I want to know if
32   it's a boy or a girl. I've only known for a few hours and
33   already I think of it as a little person. A real baby.
34   STACY: Lots of single women raise children by themselves.
35   DENISE: Not when they're sixteen. That wouldn't be best for

1   the baby. I'm not ready. I wouldn't be a good parent. Not yet.
2 STACY: You could put it up for adoption. There are lots of
3   couples like your parents' friends who would be thrilled
4   to adopt your baby.
5 DENISE: Would I be able to do it? Could I actually hand over
6   my baby to a stranger?
7 STACY: You could if you decide that's the best option. And
8   it wouldn't be a stranger; it would be someone from an
9   adoption agency. It would be a social worker that you
10   know.
11 DENISE: Two weeks ago, all I wanted for Christmas was a
12   compact disc player. Now all I want is to not be pregnant.
13 STACY: There are some things even Santa can't manage.
14
15
16
17
18
19
20
21
22
23
24
25
26
27
28
29
30
31
32
33
34
35

40

THE LAST DAY OF SCHOOL: TWO VIEWPOINTS

1   *CAST:* Two players, BRUCE and CHARLEY.

2   This is not a true dialog; it is two monologs delivered at the

3   same time, with the speakers alternating lines.

4   *AT RISE:* BRUCE and CHARLEY are On Stage at start. They

5   speak to the audience, not to each other. They act as if they do

6   not hear each other.

7

8   BRUCE: Finally! The last day of ninth grade. I thought today

9   would never come.

10 CHARLEY: Another school year is almost over. Where did

11   the time go?

12 BRUCE: Every year the days drag worse than the year before.

13 CHARLEY: It seems like football practice barely got started

14   and, all of a sudden, we're finishing up track and basketball.

15 BRUCE: Biology was the worst. Who needs to know all that

16   junk? And English! What could be more boring than books

17   that were written one hundred years ago?

18 CHARLEY: Biology was the hardest class I ever had—but I

19   learned a lot. English, too. I didn't think I'd like reading

20   those old books by Mark Twain, but they were great. I

21   suppose that's why they're still popular, a century later.

22 BRUCE: Why don't they ever teach us anything useful, like

23   how to balance a checkbook?

24 CHARLEY: The lifestyles class was my favorite. We learned

25   to compare prices and how to apply for a loan and lots of

26   other practical skills. Too bad more kids didn't sign up

27   for it. They should make lifestyles class required, instead

28   of optional.

29 BRUCE: It's raining again. You might know it would rain on

30   the last day of school and spoil the class picnic.

31 CHARLEY: Looks like the class picnic will have to be in the

32   gym this year. It's a good thing we made an alternate plan.

33 BRUCE: Plan B says, "If it rains, the picnic will be held in the

1   gym." How can we have a picnic in the gym? Picnics are
2   supposed to be outside.
3 CHARLEY: At least we won't have to worry about ants in the
4   potato salad.
5 BRUCE: My picture in the annual is terrible. Why didn't I get
6   my hair cut?
7 CHARLEY: The annuals are the best ever. They have pictures
8   of the school play and the young authors' conference, and
9   there's a terrific shot of the basketball team getting the
10   trophy for good sportsmanship.
11 BRUCE: That picture makes me look like a cross between
12   Count Dracula and an Old English sheep dog.
13 CHARLEY: Some day I'll show this to my grandchildren, to
14   prove that I didn't always have wrinkles.
15 BRUCE: I don't know why I even buy an annual. Every year,
16   it's the same old garbage.
17 CHARLEY: Maybe next year I'll offer to help with the annual.
18   It must be really satisfying to produce a book that means
19   so much to everyone.
20 BRUCE: I suppose all the kids will be getting autographs from
21   their friends, as usual. What a waste of time. Nobody ever
22   writes anything clever or original. They all say the same
23   thing: "Have a good summer."
24 CHARLEY: Someday we'll look back at these annuals and read
25   what our friends wrote to us and remember how much fun
26   school was.
27 BRUCE: How can I have a good summer when I'm stuck going
28   to summer school? I planned to sleep in every morning,
29   but, oh no, my folks insisted that I take some stupid com-
30   puter class that shoots practically my whole day.
31 CHARLEY: Always before on the last day of school, I won-
32   dered what I was going to do for the next three months.
33   This year, I signed up for a six-week summer school com-
34   puter course. It's three hours every morning, and I get a
35   full semester credit, and I'll still have all afternoon free to

1   play tennis or go swimming.
2 BRUCE: I'm so glad to be finished with Mr. Shelton and the
3   rest. If I never see another teacher again, it would be fine
4   with me.
5 CHARLEY: Maybe I'll ask a couple of the teachers to sign my
6   annual, too.
7 BRUCE: I should have complained to the principal about Mr.
8   Shelton. Isn't there some kind of a law against psycholog-
9   ical abuse? Where does he get off telling me if I want to
10   make it in the world, I'd better change my attitude? There's
11   nothing wrong with my attitude.
12 CHARLEY: Mr. Shelton. I'll ask Mr. Shelton to sign my annual.
13   Everyone complains how tough he is and calls him Mr.
14   Skeleton, but I didn't think biology was *that* bad, and Mr.
15   Shelton always volunteered to chaperone our dances.
16 BRUCE: The last day of school. Three more hours and then
17   I'm out of here.
18 CHARLEY: The last day of school. You know, I kind of hate
19   to see it end.
20
21
22
23
24
25
26
27
28
29
30
31
32
33
34
35

Playlets

41

HEARTBEATS

1 **CAST:** Three males, three females: DON, WESLEY, ED, EVELYN,
2 JUDY, SHIRLEY.
3 **SETTING:** No special setting necessary. If possible, all actors
4 should wear long-sleeved shirts, cotton gloves, and aprons. All
5 are splattered with oil.
6 *(All enter together, obviously weary.)*
7
8 EVELYN: I have never been so tired in my life.
9 DON: Me either. How long have you been here?
10 EVELYN: Ten hours. I was only supposed to work a six-hour
11 shift, but I couldn't leave when there were so many birds
12 that needed help.
13 JUDY: Same here. Reading about the oil spill in the news-
14 paper did not give me a clue to the horror of it.
15 ED: I know what you mean. I saw a newscast on TV that
16 showed all the birds—that's why I came to volunteer—but
17 even seeing it on television didn't prepare me to actually
18 hold a trembling, frightened bird in my two hands. And I
19 sure wasn't prepared to have to pry open its beak and
20 insert a feeding tube.
21 WESLEY: I could actually feel their hearts beating. Rapid at
22 first, beating fast with fear, and then gradually slowing
23 as they received food.
24 SHIRLEY: That's what I didn't expect: the fear. Their fear is
25 a threat to them now—maybe even more than the oil.
26 DON: Tell me about it. One bird pecked me on the wrist so
27 hard it drew blood. Got its beak right between my glove
28 and my shirt sleeve.
29 EVELYN: You should sing to them. Croon a soft little song,
30 like a mother rocking her baby to sleep.
31 DON: I learned that later, after I got pecked.
32 JUDY: There are so many of them. We work until we can
33 hardly see straight and it still isn't enough.

1   SHIRLEY: It's better than nothing. I had to scrub most of
2   them with a soapy toothbrush, the oil was so thick. All
3   day, I kept telling myself if I wasn't doing this, the birds
4   would die.
5   JUDY: I used cotton swabs to go around the rims of their
6   eyelids. I could tell they hated it but it had to be done.
7   Imagine having black oil in your eyes. *(She shudders.)*
8   SHIRLEY: When I first got here, I intended to count how many
9   I cleaned. I thought I'd be able to do a hundred birds or
10   even more in one day. But they were such a mess! Some
11   of them didn't even look like birds when I started on them.
12   If I had seen them somewhere else, I would have thought
13   they were just a tarry mound of feathers. It took me at
14   least an hour to do each bird.
15   ED: It's a good thing the feeding goes faster than that or they'd
16   starve to death waiting their turn.
17   EVELYN: What was that stuff you were feeding them?
18   DON: Something called trout chow. It's mixed with vegetable
19   oil and Gatorade. All whirled together in a blender until
20   it's smooth enough to slip right down their throats.
21   JUDY: Yuck. It sounds terrible.
22   WESLEY: The birds don't complain.
23   SHIRLEY: Have you gone out to see the testing ponds?
24   DON: Not yet.
25   ED: I haven't had time.
26   EVELYN: What testing ponds?
27   SHIRLEY: It's where they take the liveliest birds, after
28   they've been cleaned and fed. It's a test, to see if they might
29   be able to make it on their own. If there's any oil or soap
30   residue on their feathers, the birds can't float. They can't
31   fly, either. They can't even stay warm.
32   EVELYN: So they put them in the ponds awhile, to make sure
33   they're OK before they get released?
34   SHIRLEY: That's right. I went out there yesterday and there
35   was a whole group of them swimming around. It was a

1   thrill, knowing that without our volunteer clean-up group,

2   none of those birds would have lived.

3 DON: Five hundred thousand gallons of oil. And that's just

4   this time. How many oil spills have there been?

5 JUDY: How many more will there be?

6 ED: When I see all of these terrified, suffering wild birds, it

7   makes me almost ashamed to be a human.

8 EVELYN: I suppose that's why we're here. We're trying to

9   make amends because our species has caused such suffer-

10   ing to these other species.

11 SHIRLEY: I'm going home. If I don't get some sleep, I won't

12   be able to lift another bird.

13 JUDY: Are you coming again tomorrow?

14 ALL OTHERS: Yes. *(They smile and nod at each other.)*

15 DON: How could I stay away, now that I know how bad it is?

16 WESLEY: As long as I live, I'll remember how those heart-

17   beats feel.

18 ED: Pounding with fear in the palms of our hands. *(All exit.)*

19

20

21

22

23

24

25

26

27

28

29

30

31

32

33

34

35

42

DEAR BILL/
DEAR ASHLEY

1   *CAST:*   Two males, two females. BILL, JIM, ASHLEY, SUSAN.

2   *AT RISE:*   BILL and JIM stand together at one side of playing area.

3   ASHLEY and SUSAN stand together on the other side.

4   ASHLEY and BILL each hold a writing tablet and a pencil.

5

6   ASHLEY: This is the hardest letter I've ever written. He is

7   going to be absolutely crushed.

8   BILL: I feel like a rat. Maybe I shouldn't write at all.

9   JIM: You can't do that. That would be harder on her than

10   knowing the truth.

11   SUSAN: Just be honest with him. If Bill's as nice as you say

12   he is, he'll understand.

13   ASHLEY: He is nice. Or at least he was. I can hardly re-

14   member what he's like. Isn't that incredible? When we

15   moved, I thought I'd never forget Bill. I planned to go back

16   to Iowa after I graduate and attend college with him. I

17   thought—I really thought some day Bill and I would get

18   married. And now, only eight months later, I can hardly

19   remember him.

20   BILL: "Dear Ashley: Sorry I haven't written for awhile, but

21   I've been super busy."

22   JIM: With Melissa.

23   BILL: I can see you're going to be a big help.

24   ASHLEY: Absence is supposed to make the heart grow fon-

25   der. I must have a character flaw.

26   SUSAN: It's perfectly natural to make new friends. Bill

27   wouldn't want you to spend the rest of your high school

28   career moping around, being lonesome for him. He prob-

29   ably wants you to date other guys.

30   ASHLEY: No way. We promised each other that distance

31   wouldn't make any difference. We swore we'd always love

32   each other, no matter how long it was before we were

33   together again. This is going to break his heart.

1   JIM: Maybe she'll be relieved. Maybe she wants to go out with
2   somebody else, too, and is afraid of letting you down.
3   BILL: Are you kidding? She's still planning for us to go to
4   college together. We even talked about—about being to-
5   gether permanently.
6   JIM: So, tell her you changed your mind. Tell her you decided
7   not to go to college, after all. Say you're going to drop out
8   of school and become a beach bum.
9   BILL: I can't lie to Ashley. I'll get right to the point and tell her
10   the truth. *(He starts to write again.)* "I need to tell you some-
11   thing, and I wish you were here so I could do it in person,
12   except if you were here I wouldn't have to tell you this."
13   JIM: Maybe you should call her.
14   SUSAN: I moved when I was in the fourth grade. My best
15   friend, Missy, and I swore we'd write every day. I got two
16   letters from her.
17   ASHLEY: That's terrible.
18   SUSAN: I agree. She got *three* letters from me.
19   ASHLEY: That was fourth grade. You expect kids in fourth
20   grade to forget.
21   SUSAN: Do you want me to write the letter for you? "Dear
22   Bill: I've been lonely and, even though I haven't met any-
23   one I like as much as you, I've decided to date other guys.
24   I hope you'll understand and feel free to go out, too." There.
25   All written. All you have to do is put it on paper.
26   ASHLEY: That isn't exactly true. I have met someone else.
27   That's the problem.
28   SUSAN: "Dear Bill: I met this terrific guy named Kevin, and
29   we're practically going steady. Just thought you'd like to
30   know."
31   ASHLEY: You know what really bothers me about this whole
32   thing? What if I keep doing this? What if, every time I meet
33   a new guy I think I'm in love and then a few months later
34   I change my mind? I'll be one of those people with eight
35   divorces.

1   **BILL:**   What if she tries to kill herself?
2   **JIM:**   She won't. I never saw her act the least depressed.
3   **BILL:**   She never got jilted before.
4   **JIM:**   She's too smart to let one disappointment ruin her whole
5   life.
6   **BILL:**   *(Writing again)* "I will always care about you, and I hope
7   we can stay friends."
8   **JIM:**   Even though you probably hate me right at this moment.
9   **SUSAN:**   Pretend I'm Bill. Say it to me.
10   **ASHLEY:**   I'm sorry to hurt you, but I have to be honest and
11   tell you I've been dating somebody else. I hope you'll try
12   to understand.
13   **SUSAN:**   Perfect. Write it down. *(ASHLEY writes.)*
14   **JIM:**   It isn't fair, you know. You're worried about how to get
15   rid of an extra girlfriend, and I've never gone out with
16   anyone.
17   **BILL:**   Why don't you write to Ashley? Maybe you and she . . .
18   **JIM:**   Forget it. I want a girlfriend that's here in the flesh. Lots
19   of nice, curvy flesh.
20   **BILL:**   Like Melissa.
21   **ASHLEY:**   There. It's done.
22   **SUSAN:**   Just in time. Here comes Kevin.
23   **ASHLEY:**   *(Waves)* Hi, Kevin. *(She runs Off Stage.)*
24   **BILL:**   *(Hands letter to JIM.)* Could you mail this for me? I'm
25   supposed to meet Melissa, and I'm already late. *(He exits.)*
26   **SUSAN:**   Poor Bill.
27   **JIM:**   Poor Ashley.
28
29
30
31
32
33
34
35

43

ONE EVERY
TWENTY-TWO MINUTES

1   *CAST:* Four players: BECKY, TODD, JAMES, ANITA.

2   BECKY and TODD are ghosts. They have white sheets draped

3   over their heads and (optional) white face makeup. They cannot

4   speak; JAMES and ANITA cannot see them. However, the

5   ghosts react to what JAMES and ANITA say.

6   *AT RISE:* BECKY and TODD enter, from opposite sides. They

7   move slowly, as if floating. They do not see each other. Before

8   they reach the center of the playing area, they stop and face

9   the audience.

10   *(JAMES and ANITA enter, talking, and go forward until they*

11   *are standing in between the ghosts.)*

12

13 ANITA: I just can't believe it. Yesterday, Becky and I were

14   making plans to go on a camping trip this summer. Now

15   she's dead.

16 JAMES: Two friends in one week.

17 ANITA: I had never been to a funeral until I went to Todd's.

18   It was the hardest thing I ever did, and now there'll be

19   another one.

20 JAMES: I keep thinking about what the minister said at

21   Todd's service—that every twenty-two minutes a teenager

22   is killed as a result of drunken driving. When I heard that,

23   it seemed like an exaggeration. I'm sixteen years old, and

24   Todd was the first person I ever knew who was killed by

25   a drunk driver. But now, just a week later, Becky is gone.

26   It's as if the statistics are making up for the years when I

27   didn't lose any friends.

28 ANITA: It makes you wonder who's next.

29 JAMES: Exactly.

30 ANITA: It seems even worse this time.

31 JAMES: How could it be?

32 ANITA: Because it wasn't Becky's fault. With Todd, it was at

33   least partly his own fault. *(TODD cringes and grimaces.)*

1   JAMES: Todd didn't want to die. *(TODD vigorously shakes his*
2   *head no.)*
3   ANITA: Of course not. But he *had* been drinking.
4   JAMES: Just beer. At a private party. Todd wasn't a big
5   boozer.
6   ANITA: I don't mean to talk against Todd. I liked Todd a lot.
7   I had a secret crush on him all through seventh grade.
8   *(TODD and BECKY look amazed. TODD points to himself, as*
9   *if to say, "On me?" He is pleased by this news.)* **But no matter**
10   how much we liked him, the fact is he had been drinking
11   that night and then he lost control of the car on his way
12   home. *(TODD hangs his head.)* **It's hard to blame anyone**
13   but Todd for the fact that he was killed.
14   JAMES: Todd would never have committed suicide. *(TODD*
15   *again shakes his head no.)*
16   ANITA: Not with pills or a gun, but the result is the same.
17   JAMES: Yes, I guess it is. And it's the same for his family. I
18   went over to Todd's house to return a book I had borrowed
19   from him. His mother couldn't even talk to me. All she did
20   was cry. *(TODD covers his ears, unable to bear it.)*
21   ANITA: It's terrible for Becky's family, too. Becky didn't
22   drink. It's so unfair that she should die this way. *(BECKY*
23   *hugs herself and rocks back and forth in sorrow.)* **She was**
24   walking across the street, with a green light, on her way
25   to a baby-sitting job.
26   JAMES: How could that woman not see a red light at 5 o'clock
27   in the afternoon? How could she not see a person in the
28   middle of the crosswalk? That lady is going to have the
29   book thrown at her in court.
30   ANITA: That won't bring Becky back. *(BECKY stops rocking.*
31   *She looks up, slowly shaking her head no.)* **And the worst of**
32   it is, that woman had already been arrested once before
33   for drunken driving.
34   JAMES: I was thinking of asking Becky to go out with me. I
35   was trying to get up my nerve to ask her. *(BECKY reacts*

1   *with surprise and pleasure.)*

2   **ANITA:**   She would have said yes. I know she would. *(BECKY*

3   *nods her head yes. She smiles.)*

4   **JAMES:**   Well, it's too late now. *(BECKY's smile fades.)* I've felt

5   weird ever since I first heard about Todd. I know accidents

6   happen and I know people die, but, somehow, until now,

7   it just never seemed like the one person every twenty-two

8   minutes would be someone I know.

9   **ANITA:**   Or you.

10   **JAMES:**   Or me.

11   **ANITA:**   It makes me feel vulnerable.

12   **JAMES:**   It made me decide not to drink anymore. *(TODD raises*

13   *a fist in congratulations.)*

14   **ANITA:**   Becky didn't drink, either. *(BECKY shrugs helplessly.)*

15   **JAMES:**   I'm going to miss both of them.

16   **ANITA:**   Yes. And think how much *they* are going to miss.

17   **JAMES:**   Graduation.

18   **ANITA:**   College.

19   **JAMES:**   Careers. Todd wanted to do work with artificial intel-

20   ligence. He was a whiz with computers.

21   **ANITA:**   Becky wanted to be a lawyer.

22   **JAMES:**   Marriage.

23   **ANITA:**   Kids.

24   **JAMES:**   Everything. *(During the next two lines, ANITA and*

25   *JAMES exit. Ghosts watch them leave.)*

26   **ANITA:**   Everything. They are going to miss the whole rest of

27   their lives.

28   **JAMES:**   The whole rest of their lives. *(BECKY and TODD slowly*

29   *turn and move Off Stage, the same way they came in.)*

30

31

32

33

34

35

44

SISTERLY LOVE

1   *CAST:* Three sisters: ALLISON, TRUDY, JEAN. JEAN is
2   youngest.
3   *SETTING:* Minimal—any room in family home. Need only a couple
4   of chairs and a telephone.
5   *(ALLISON and TRUDY are On Stage at start of scene.)*
6
7   ALLISON: Here she comes. Don't forget—no matter what she
8   says or does, we pretend we don't hear her or see her.
9   TRUDY: This is really going to get to her. Especially if Sue
10   remembers to call in a few minutes.
11   ALLISON: Maybe it will teach her a lesson about blabbing
12   other people's secrets. Especially ours.
13   TRUDY: Shh. *(JEAN enters.)*
14   JEAN: Hi. What are you guys doing?
15   ALLISON: And then Mr. Hammer assigned two book reports
16   for this week.
17   JEAN: I did a book report last week.
18   TRUDY: I don't mind book reports, as long as they're written.
19   JEAN: How come you have to do two in one week?
20   ALLISON: I agree. Oral reports make me nervous.
21   JEAN: Mine was oral. I got a B. I would have had an A, but
22   I talked too long.
23   ALLISON: I'm going to the library. Do you want to come?
24   TRUDY: Sure. I always like to go to the library.
25   JEAN: Me, too. I'll go with you.
26   ALLISON: Let's ride our bikes.
27   TRUDY: Great idea. My thighs need the exercise.
28   JEAN: What about me? Mom won't let me ride that far yet. I
29   have to walk with someone or take the bus.
30   TRUDY: I'll take my tote bag; it fits on the bike carrier.
31   JEAN: What about me? I want to go with you.
32   ALLISON: We'd better leave a note, so Mom knows where we
33   are.

1   TRUDY: It's a good thing Jean isn't here. She'd want to tag
2   along.
3   JEAN: I *am* here. I'm standing right next to you.
4   ALLISON: I wonder where she is. She's usually home by now.
5   TRUDY: Maybe she went home with Jennifer.
6   JEAN: What's the matter with you? Are you blind and deaf
7   all of a sudden?
8   ALLISON: Actually, it's rather nice without her. For once we
9   can talk without worrying that she's going to eavesdrop
10   and then blab everything we say to anyone who'll listen.
11   JEAN: I don't do that!
12   TRUDY: Our sister, the spy.
13   ALLISON: Of course, she's younger than we are.
14   TRUDY: When she's more mature, maybe she'll learn to keep
15   her mouth shut.
16   JEAN: I am mature. And if you guys don't quit ignoring me,
17   I'm going to tell Mom.
18   ALLISON: Have you read any good books lately? Something
19   I would like? I may as well do my reports on books that
20   are interesting.
21   TRUDY: I haven't read anything but my biology text for
22   weeks.
23   JEAN: I read one called *Sisters, Long Ago*. It was good.
24   ALLISON: That's why I didn't take biology. Too much
25   memorizing.
26   JEAN: You guys are ignoring me on purpose, aren't you?
27   TRUDY: I'll look for a novel at the library. I need a break
28   from biology.
29   JEAN: You think if you pretend I'm not here, I'll leave. *(The*
30   *phone rings. ALLISON answers.)*
31   ALLISON: Hello? No, she isn't here. Can I take a message?
32   JEAN: Is that for me?
33   ALLISON: I don't know when she'll be back. She isn't home
34   from school yet.
35   JEAN: *(She grabs for phone.)* Give me that. *(ALLISON hangs up.)*

1   That was for me, wasn't it?
2   TRUDY: Who was it?
3   ALLISON: Somebody for Jean.
4   JEAN: I knew it. I knew it was for me.
5   TRUDY: Probably Jennifer.
6   ALLISON: It was a boy.
7   JEAN: A boy? A boy called for me, and you said I wasn't
8   here? When Mom gets home, you guys are going to be in
9   big trouble.
10   TRUDY: Maybe we should run next door and tell the
11   Smithburg kids that Jean got a phone call from a boy.
12   JEAN: Don't you dare!
13   ALLISON: That's what she would do, if the call had been for
14   one of us.
15   JEAN: Once. Just once I told the Smithburgs.
16   TRUDY: Let's do it.
17   JEAN: No! Kevin Smithburg is in my class. He'll tell the whole
18   school. No boy will ever call me again.
19   ALLISON: While we're at it, let's be sure to write to Uncle Bill
20   and tell him, too.
21   TRUDY: Good idea. That way, the next time he talks to Dad,
22   he can mention that he understands Jean has a boyfriend,
23   and Dad can have an anxiety attack.
24   JEAN: I didn't write to Uncle Bill. He called and I happened
25   to answer the phone, and when he asked me what was
26   new, I couldn't think of anything else to say.
27   ALLISON: Let's go. I want enough time at the library, and it
28   may take awhile at the Smithburgs'.
29   JEAN: *(On the verge of tears)* No!
30   TRUDY: Let's wait and go over there after we get back.
31   Kevin's at basketball practice now. *(TRUDY and ALLISON*
32   *rise and start to leave. JEAN suddenly gasps and clutches her*
33   *chest. She collapses on the floor. TRUDY and ALLISON rush*
34   *to her and kneel beside her.)* What's wrong? What happened?
35   ALLISON: Maybe she had a heart attack. *(JEAN is unrespon-*

1   *sive, eyes closed.)* **You don't think we upset her so much she**
2   **had a heart attack, do you?**
3   **TRUDY:**   **I'm going to call 9-1-1.** *(She grabs telephone.)*
4   **ALLISON:**   **What if she's just acting? What if she's pretending**
5   **she's sick to get even with us for ignoring her?**
6   **TRUDY:**   *(Hesitates)* **What if she isn't pretending?**
7   **ALLISON:**   **Call 9-1-1. I'll do CPR.** *(TRUDY starts to dial. ALLI-*
8   *SON tilts JEAN's head back and sticks her finger in JEAN's*
9   *mouth.)*
10   **JEAN:**   *(Turns her head away)* **Blah. Get your hand out of my**
11   **mouth.** *(TRUDY quickly hangs up. ALLISON jumps to her feet.)*
12   **TRUDY:**   **You little fake!**
13   **JEAN:**   *(Stands)* **Me? You're calling me a fake? You've been**
14   **pretending all day that you couldn't see me or hear me.**
15   **ALLISON:**   **We should have left her lying on the floor.**
16   **TRUDY:**   **Next time, we will.**
17   **JEAN:**   **There isn't going to be any next time. I'm never talking**
18   **to either of you again.**
19   **TRUDY:**   **Good.**
20   **ALLISON:**   **Wait till Mom gets home and finds out you faked**
21   **a heart attack and let us call 9-1-1. That's just as bad as a**
22   **false fire alarm.**
23   **JEAN:**   **You didn't call. You stopped before they answered.**
24   **ALLISON:**   **Only because you didn't want my finger in your**
25   **mouth. If I hadn't done that, you would have let an ambu-**
26   **lance come. Probably some old man would have died be-**
27   **cause all the medics were over here and couldn't help him**
28   **in time.**
29   **JEAN:**   **If you tell Mom that, I'll tell her why I had to do it. I'll**
30   **tell her about my phone call. I'll tell her everything you did.**
31   **TRUDY:**   **You will anyway. You always do. You follow us**
32   **around like a private investigator, and then you blab every**
33   **detail to anyone who'll listen.**
34   **JEAN:**   *(Starts to cry)* **If you would include me once in awhile,**
35   **maybe I wouldn't.** *(ALLISON and TRUDY look at each other,*

1   *surprised by this remark.)* **It's always two against one, and**
2   **I'm the one. How do you think I feel when I'm treated like**
3   **an outcast by my own family? No matter where you're**
4   **going, if I want to go, too, you say no. You act like I have**
5   **a contagious disease or like I'm some kind of freak and**
6   **you're ashamed to be seen with me.**
7   ALLISON: Oh, come on. It isn't that bad.
8   JEAN: Yes, it is. I can't help it that I'm younger than you. You
9   always have each other, and I never have anybody.
10   TRUDY: You have Jennifer. *(She gets tissue and hands it to Jean.)*
11   JEAN: That isn't the same. She doesn't live here.
12   ALLISON: You have to admit, you do follow us around and
13   listen to what we say.
14   JEAN: I just want to be with you. I want you to like me.
15   TRUDY: We do like you.
16   JEAN: No you don't.
17   ALLISON: If we didn't, we wouldn't have tried to help when
18   we thought you were sick.
19   JEAN: I won't repeat anything you say, ever again.
20   TRUDY: Promise?
21   JEAN: Promise.
22   ALLISON: And you won't tattle to Mom and Dad all the time?
23   JEAN: Never.
24   ALLISON: OK. You can go to the library with us. We'll walk.
25   JEAN: Who called for me?
26   ALLISON: Nobody called for you.
27   JEAN: You said a boy called for me. Did he give his name?
28   TRUDY: It wasn't a boy. It was Sue.
29   JEAN: Allison answered. She said it was a boy and he asked
30   for me.
31   ALLISON: It was Sue. We told her to call.
32   JEAN: *(Stares at them for a second, stunned, as she realizes what*
33   *really happened)* **That's the meanest trick I ever heard of!**
34   **I'm telling Mom!**
35   TRUDY: Are you? *(They all look at each other.)*

1 JEAN: No.
2 ALLISON: Let's go.
3 JEAN: Actually, if you had done that to anyone but me, I
4   would think it was funny.
5 TRUDY: Maybe she really is getting mature.
6 ALLISON: Finally. *(They exit together.)*
7
8
9
10
11
12
13
14
15
16
17
18
19
20
21
22
23
24
25
26
27
28
29
30
31
32
33
34
35

45

WIN, LOSE OR LEARN

1   *CAST:*   Four players: MATT, STEVE, TONY, RICKY.

2   No special setting necessary.

3   *(MATT, STEVE and TONY are On Stage as scene opens.)*

4

5   MATT: We could have beat them. If Coach Girard had let the

6   first string finish the game, we would have won.

7   STEVE: No question. We had them. But, oh no, Coach had to

8   let everybody have their turn to play.

9   MATT: It's the most stupid coaching policy I've ever heard

10   of. You don't see professional coaches making sure every

11   player has a chance to play in every game.

12   STEVE: I couldn't believe it when he took me out and put

13   Ricky Schuster in. Ricky Schuster hasn't made a free

14   throw the entire season. He just barely made the team.

15   MATT: Maybe Coach had a big bet on this game. Maybe he

16   has a secret gambling problem, and he had to make sure

17   we lost so he could collect the money and pay his debts.

18   TONY: Oh, come on, Matt. You know that isn't true. He just

19   feels strongly that every person on the team should get

20   some playing time. If you were a sub instead of being on

21   the starting team, you'd probably like his policy.

22   MATT: Not if it meant we had to lose the biggest game of the

23   season by two points. Two lousy points! And all because

24   the worst players on the entire squad got to play the last

25   five minutes.

26   TONY: Those guys come to practice every day. They work

27   just as hard as we do.

28   STEVE: Sure, they come to practice. But that doesn't make

29   them good players. At least, not good enough to go in for

30   the final five minutes of the most important game of the

31   season.

32   MATT: My dad is going to have a fit. The last time we lost a

33   game because of this dumb rule, Dad threatened to com-

1   plain to the school board. This time, he'll do it. I know he
2   will. I could hear him booing.
3   STEVE: Maybe the school board will overrule Coach.
4   MATT: Or fire him.
5   TONY: Is that what you want? You told me Coach Girard has
6   done more to help you improve your game than any other
7   coach you've ever had.
8   MATT: I'm not saying he's a bad coach. I'm just saying he
9   has a rotten philosophy about who gets to play. What's so
10   important about sending Ricky Schuster in for five min-
11   utes so he can miss two free throws, double dribble, and
12   throw the ball straight into the hands of the other team's
13   center?
14   TONY: Shhh. Here comes Ricky. He'll hear you. *(He points.*
15   *MATT and STEVE look. RICKY enters.)*
16   RICKY: Hi, guys.
17   OTHERS: Hi, Ricky.
18   RICKY: Sorry about the game.
19   TONY: Yeah.
20   RICKY: I wanted to play my best today. My grandparents
21   came over a hundred miles just to see the game. I was
22   really hoping I'd make those free throws.
23   MATT: So were we.
24   TONY: Maybe next time.
25   MATT: I doubt it.
26   RICKY: It's so frustrating. At home, I practice free throws,
27   and I sink eighty percent of them. Swish! Straight through
28   the net. Then I get in a tight game, and I don't know what
29   happens.
30   MATT: I do. You miss.
31   TONY: Lay off, Matt. He feels bad enough.
32   RICKY: At least I got in for a few minutes. I would have really
33   felt terrible if Grandpa and Grandma came so far to watch
34   me play and then I never even got in the game.
35   MATT: Don't they care that your team lost?

1   RICKY: Well, naturally, they'd like to see us win. But they
2   agree with Coach Girard's philosophy that the important
3   thing is for each player to try to play up to his best poten-
4   tial. If you win, that's icing on the cake.
5   STEVE: Was today your best potential?
6   RICKY: No way. Coach says I need more experience. He says
7   my coordination was slow to develop, but if I keep practic-
8   ing, I'll be a good player someday.
9   MATT: Someday. What happens in the meantime?
10   STEVE: It's great to get practice, but does it have to come
11   when we're tied with five minutes to go?
12   TONY: Hey! He said he was sorry about the game.
13   RICKY: I need practice under pressure, too. So do the other
14   subs. We have to know how it feels.
15   MATT: Well, I'd like to know how it feels to win a game.
16   TONY: We've won some games. Six wins, four losses.
17   STEVE: It could have been eight wins and two losses.
18   MATT: My dad is really going to chew me out tonight.
19   RICKY: For what? You played a great game.
20   MATT: Most of the time. But I missed both of those long shots,
21   the three-pointers. If I'd made either one of them, we would
22   have won.
23   TONY: You aren't the only person who missed a shot.
24   RICKY: That's for sure.
25   MATT: I guess you'll really get yelled at when you get home.
26   RICKY: No. If I do something good, my folks tell me it was
27   great. If I play lousy, like today, they just say it was fun
28   to come and watch the game.
29   TONY: That's how my mom is, too. She says as long as I play
30   clean, she's proud of me.
31   RICKY: Well, I have to get going. My grandparents are taking
32   the whole family out for pizza. See you at practice tomor-
33   row. *(RICKY exits.)*
34   MATT: Unfortunately.
35

46

THE SIMPLE LIFE

1 *CAST:* Three players: EMMA, KATE, SHELLY.

2 *SETTING:* A table and three chairs in school cafeteria.

3 *AT RISE:* EMMA, KATE and SHELLY enter, carrying lunch trays,

4   and sit at a table, facing audience. SHELLY has a can of pop;

5   KATE has a carton of milk; EMMA has a glass of water. Other

6   food optional. EMMA opens her tote bag and removes a cloth

7   napkin.

8

9 EMMA: Thanks for asking me to eat lunch with you. I was

10   really nervous about my first day at this school.

11 KATE: I moved last year, so I know what it feels like.

12 SHELLY: Did either of you watch the special on Channel 4

13   last night—"The Feast of the Eyeball Eaters?"

14 KATE: I saw the first half, but my mom said it was too violent

15   and made me turn it off. I watched a rerun instead.

16 SHELLY: Oh, too bad. The end was the best part. I could

17   hardly stand to look at it. Did you see it, Emma?

18 EMMA: No.

19 SHELLY: *(To EMMA)* You didn't get anything to drink.

20 EMMA: I have water.

21 SHELLY: You can get Coke or Pepsi from the machine, if you

22   don't want milk.

23 EMMA: No, thanks. I don't drink pop.

24 KATE: Never? *(EMMA shakes her head no.)*

25 SHELLY: Why not? Are you allergic?

26 EMMA: My family tries to live as simply as possible. We don't

27   buy anything unless we need it.

28 KATE: Did your parents lose their jobs? Is that why you moved?

29 EMMA: Oh, no. They both work. We moved so they would be

30   closer to their jobs. My dad rides his bike to work now.

31 SHELLY: I don't get it. If your parents both work, why can't

32   you afford to buy pop?

33 EMMA: It isn't that I can't afford to. It's that I choose not to.

1   My family decided a couple of years ago that we would
2   try not to waste any of the earth's resources. We had to
3   make a lot of changes, and at first I didn't like all of them
4   but now I do.
5 SHELLY: Changes like not drinking pop?
6 EMMA: Right. Water is cheaper, better for my health, and it
7   doesn't waste energy.
8 SHELLY: *(Defensively)* I recycle my pop cans.
9 EMMA: I'm not criticizing you. I'm just explaining my way.
10 KATE: What else did you give up, besides soft drinks?
11 EMMA: The main things were appliances, like the dishwasher
12   and the clothes dryer. I don't use a hair dryer anymore,
13   either, or a curling iron. That's why I keep my hair short.
14 SHELLY: It's cute that way.
15 EMMA: Thanks. It's easy.
16 KATE: It takes me half an hour every morning to dry and
17   curl my hair.
18 SHELLY: It sounds like your family wants to live in the past,
19   before people had labor-saving machines.
20 EMMA: The machines that save labor use electrical energy.
21   We prefer to use people power. And when appliances like
22   dryers wear out, they usually end up in land fills.
23 KATE: You said your dad rides a bike to work. Don't you
24   have a car, either?
25 EMMA: We have a car, but we don't use it much. My mom
26   takes the bus to work.
27 SHELLY: What kind of work do they do?
28 EMMA: Mom's a physical therapist; Dad's an engineer. But
29   they both work only part time. We don't need as much
30   money, now that we live simply, and they wanted time for
31   other things. They have a big garden and lots of hobbies.
32 SHELLY: My folks both work full time, and we still never
33   have any extra money.
34 KATE: Neither do we.
35 EMMA: We used to be that way, too. But you'd be surprised

1   how much money you don't spend when you cut out things
2   that aren't essential.
3 SHELLY: Don't you ever do anything fun?
4 EMMA: All the time. We go camping, and we work in a com-
5   munity theatre group. Next week we start rehearsals for
6   "Dracula, Darling." I'm going to help with props.
7 KATE: I'd like that.
8 EMMA: It's fun. Mom has a part this time, but sometimes she
9   works backstage, too. Dad's usually the stage manager.
10 SHELLY: I suppose you watch TV a lot. That's cheap.
11 EMMA: We don't have a TV.
12 SHELLY: Do you belong to some weird religion?
13 KATE: Shelly! That's rude.
14 EMMA: I know it seems strange when you first think about
15   it. Living a simple life means not having a lot of things
16   that other people take for granted, like TV and personal
17   computers and VCRs.
18 SHELLY: It sounds awful.
19 EMMA: That's what I thought, at first. But now that we've
20   done it awhile, I like the simple way better.
21 SHELLY: I'd hate it if I could never watch TV. I'd be bored
22   out of my mind. Like last night. There was absolutely noth-
23   ing to do except watch "The Feast of the Eyeball Eaters."
24 KATE: *(To Emma)* What did you do last night?
25 EMMA: I finished carving a wooden duck for my grandpa's
26   birthday present. I made it from some driftwood that I
27   found when we went clamming. And then I wrote a letter
28   to my pen pal in Japan and then Dad and I made popcorn
29   and played gin rummy.
30 KATE: It sounds a lot more interesting than the stupid rerun
31   I watched. Tonight I'm going to see if my dad wants to
32   play cards with me. Maybe my brother will play, too.
33 SHELLY: Not me. Tonight is the sequel: "Son of the Eyeball
34   Eaters." I can hardly wait. *(They stand and pick up lunch*
35   *trays. EMMA folds her cloth napkin and puts it back in her tote*

1   *bag.)* **Didn't you think the school would have napkins?**
2 **EMMA:** **I don't use paper products. It's easy to carry my own**
3   **cloth napkin. I use a cloth handkerchief, too, and I have**
4   **a water cup for times when there's nothing but paper or**
5   **Styrofoam cups.**
6 **SHELLY:** **What about toilet paper? Do you carry a rag with**
7   **you?**
8 **KATE:** **Shelly!** *(EMMA laughs.)*
9 **SHELLY:** **Well, she said she doesn't use paper products.**
10 **EMMA:** **I use the necessary ones.**
11 **SHELLY:** **That's a relief.**
12 **KATE:** **We'd better go. It's almost time for class to start.**
13 **SHELLY:** **I'll meet you after school. You still want to go to**
14   **the mall, don't you, to shop for earrings?**
15 **KATE:** **Yes.** *(She looks at EMMA.)* **Do you want to come with us?**
16 **EMMA:** **No, thanks.**
17 **SHELLY:** **I suppose you don't believe in shopping at malls.**
18 **EMMA:** **There's nothing wrong with malls, but I buy most of**
19   **my clothes at consignment shops or rummage sales.**
20 **KATE:** *(Nodding in understanding)* **We need warm clothes, not**
21   **designer jeans.**
22 **EMMA:** **I'd go with you, except I promised my neighbor I'd**
23   **babysit while she goes to the doctor. See you later.** *(She*
24   *exits.)*
25 **SHELLY:** **What a weird way to live. I wonder if she buys**
26   **second-hand underwear.**
27 **KATE:** **I wonder how many trees are used every day to make**
28   **paper napkins and paper cups.**
29 **SHELLY:** **See you after school.**
30 **KATE:** **Maybe I'll just window shop this afternoon. I don't**
31   **really need new earrings.**
32
33
34
35

47

NO EASY ANSWERS

1   *CAST:*   Seven players: LEADER, PATTY, KEVIN, BOB, BONNIE,
2   ROGER, JILL.
3   *AT RISE:*   LEADER, PATTY, KEVIN and BOB sit together on
4   right side of the playing area. There is one empty chair on the
5   left side.
6

7   **LEADER:**   **Welcome to the first meeting of Problem Solvers.**
8   **Three people will be sharing a problem with us. We have**
9   **promised not to discuss what they tell us with anyone**
10   **outside this group. Our task is to listen and to suggest**
11   **ways for them to help themselves. They ask you to be**
12   **completely honest and open in your remarks. In return,**
13   **they have agreed to accept at least one of your suggestions.**
14   *(LEADER calls Off-stage.)* **First problem, please.** *(BONNIE*
15   *enters and sits in the empty chair.)*
16   **BONNIE:**   **I never eat lunch at school. My parents don't know**
17   **this; they would have a fit if I told them. They give me**
18   **money every week to buy lunch in the cafeteria, but I**
19   **never do. The food isn't bad. It isn't the greatest, but they**
20   **have tacos and spaghetti, and there's always fruit and**
21   **salad. I could choke it down without any trouble. In fact,**
22   **some days, I'm so hungry and it smells so good that I can**
23   **hardly stand not to buy a lunch, but then I remember. No**
24   **one ever sits with me. I never eat lunch at school because**
25   **it is too awful to sit in the cafeteria alone. Not that I blame**
26   **anyone. Who would want to sit with a fat slob like me?**
27   **LEADER:**   **Why doesn't anyone sit with Bonnie?**
28   **KEVIN:**   **Because she never talks.**
29   **BOB:**   **Her whole family is strange. Her brother's a real wacko.**
30   **PATTY:**   **I thought she didn't eat lunch because she's fat and**
31   **was trying to diet.**
32   **LEADER:**   **How does she get fat if she never eats lunch?**
33   **BONNIE:**   **By the time I get home from school, I'm famished.**

1   I eat everything in sight. My mom is constantly trying to
2   get me to go on a diet. She was fat, too, until last year.
3   Then she had to have an operation, and while she was in
4   the hospital, she had a tummy tuck. Mom loves to cook.
5   She makes fantastic brownies and spaghetti. She even
6   makes cinnamon rolls, and this great dessert called pecan
7   fudge torte. I drool just thinking about it. I asked her how
8   she expected me to diet when I'm living in the temptation
9   capital of the world. She says she cooks for my dad and
10   my brother; they don't have a weight problem.
11 BOB: Man, that's unfair. Who could diet when someone else
12   is chowing down goodies in front of them all the time?
13 PATTY: Her mom is being mean.
14 LEADER: What can Bonnie do to help herself?
15 KEVIN: Eat lunch. If she ate lunch, she wouldn't be so hungry
16   when she got home, and she wouldn't pig out on her mom's
17   pecan fudge torte.
18 PATTY: But she's embarrassed to sit by herself every day.
19 BOB: She could look for someone else who's sitting alone and
20   ask them if she could sit with them.
21 KEVIN: She could bring her lunch from home and ask one
22   of the teachers if she could eat in the classroom.
23 LEADER: Bonnie thinks her problem is that no one sits with
24   her in the cafeteria. What do you think Bonnie's problem is?
25 PATTY: She's fat, and she's self-conscious about it.
26 KEVIN: Lack of friends.
27 BOB: Her mother. No, it's her whole family. I'd be weird, too,
28   if I had to live with her brother.
29 LEADER: She can't change her family. What can she change?
30 PATTY: Her weight. Nobody controls what Bonnie puts in
31   her mouth except Bonnie. If she is really determined to
32   lose the extra weight, she could do it.
33 BOB: She could go to the gym during lunch hour and work
34   out. That would help her lose weight.
35 KEVIN: Yes. She could run every day or do some other

1   aerobic-type exercise.

2   PATTY: She could use her lunch money to buy fresh fruit to

3   eat instead of her mother's fattening desserts.

4   BOB: If she got her weight under control, she'd feel more

5   positive about herself, and it might not be so hard for her

6   to make friends.

7   KEVIN: She could also find something else to do after school

8   every day, so she isn't tempted to eat.

9   BOB: Good idea. She should join a club or get a part-time job.

10   She might make a friend.

11   PATTY: She could get a paper route and either walk or ride

12   a bike to deliver the papers. That would give her something

13   to do and a way to exercise at the same time.

14   LEADER: So, your advice to Bonnie is:

15   KEVIN: Take control of what you eat.

16   PATTY: Keep busy after school.

17   BOB: Get more exercise.

18   **LEADER:**   *(Calls Off-stage)* **Second problem, please.** *(BONNIE*

19   *exits. ROGER enters.)*

20   ROGER: My problem is my older brother. Brendan is the per-

21   fect person. Every parent's dream child. He's good looking;

22   he never gets in trouble; he's a straight-A student; he's pres-

23   ident of the debate team and he already has a basketball

24   scholarship to an Ivy League college. The trouble is, every-

25   one expects me to be just like Brendan. But I'm not. I'm

26   no delinquent or anything, but I am not Mr. Teen America,

27   either. If I get mostly Bs on my report card, my parents

28   don't complain, but I can tell they're disappointed. And I'm

29   a total klutz on the basketball court. I feel like no matter

30   what I do, I'll never be as good as Brendan, so why try?

31   LEADER: What is Roger's problem?

32   BOB: It isn't his brother. His brother isn't doing anything

33   wrong.

34   PATTY: Roger's problem is himself. It's how he feels about

35   his brother.

1   KEVIN: That's right. I think Roger's envious of his brother.

2   LEADER: What can Roger do about his problem?

3   PATTY: Develop his own strengths. There must be something

4   that he's better at than his brother.

5   KEVIN: He should quit comparing himself to Brendan. He's

6   unhappy because he says everyone else compares him to

7   his brother, but he does the same thing himself.

8   BOB: He needs to let go of the jealousy.

9   PATTY: Roger should choose something he's interested in

10   and then work at getting really good at it. Music lessons,

11   maybe. Or acting. Anything that's exciting to him.

12   BOB: Something that Brendan doesn't do.

13   KEVIN: He needs to stay busy. It's a cop-out to say he

14   shouldn't bother to try because he can't compete with his

15   brother. If he's active and busy, he won't have so much

16   time to mope around and feel inadequate.

17   PATTY: He could try helping someone who's less fortunate.

18   Get involved with a charity or visit the little kids at Chil-

19   dren's Hospital. His own problem won't seem so bad when

20   he's around some kid who has leukemia.

21   LEADER: So, your advice to Roger is:

22   KEVIN: Quit comparing yourself to your brother.

23   BOB: Develop a skill all your own.

24   PATTY: Find someone who needs your help.

25   LEADER: *(Calls Off-stage)* Problem three, please. *(ROGER*

26   *exits. JILL enters.)*

27   JILL: I really don't know why I agreed to do this. The whole

28   thing is a waste of time.

29   LEADER: State your problem, please.

30   JILL: Which one?

31   LEADER: Whichever one you want help with.

32   JILL: If my problems could be fixed, I wouldn't be here. This

33   committee is a dumb idea, just like everything else that

34   goes on in this so-called institution of learning.

35   LEADER: If you don't want to state a problem, perhaps you

1   could tell us what you dislike about school.

2   JILL: Can you stay for a few weeks? Because that's how long

3   it would take.

4   LEADER: Go ahead and begin. I'll tell you when your time is

5   up.

6   JILL: Well, for starters, the teachers are all prejudiced against

7   anybody who doesn't happen to have a parent on the

8   school board. And the stuff they teach us is so unreal. Do

9   you know what we're doing in social studies this month?

10   We're learning about all the religions of the world. Talk

11   about a waste of time. I don't go to church so what possible

12   reason is there for me to know about Buddha and Con-

13   fucius? And my P.E. teacher keeps talking about "personal

14   goals." She says everyone should set personal goals and

15   then compete only with themselves. Well, the only personal

16   goal I have is to quit school and leave home and get away

17   from this backwards town.

18   LEADER: Thank you. Your time is up. *(JILL sits. During the*

19   *following discussion she makes a point of looking bored. She*

20   *reacts to the suggestions by rolling her eyes, shaking her head,*

21   *etc., to convey how pointless she thinks they are.)* **What do you**

22   think Jill's problem is?

23   PATTY: This one's easy. Her problem is her attitude.

24   KEVIN: But why? Why is she so negative? Is that the real

25   problem or just a symptom of something else?

26   BOB: Her attitude is causing her a lot of grief, so whether it's

27   the basic problem or not, we should try to help her change

28   it.

29   LEADER: How? What do you think Jill can do to help herself?

30   PATTY: Quit complaining. Try to see something positive for

31   a change.

32   KEVIN: She can choose to be happy. Maybe that's what her

33   personal goal ought to be—choosing happiness.

34   BOB: She could pretend to like school. Sometimes if you pre-

35   tend to like something, pretty soon you really do like it.

1   PATTY: I never thought of that. Maybe I could pretend to
2   like my little sister.
3   BOB: Maybe Jill could make up a plan for herself. If she is
4   serious about wanting to get away from this town, she
5   needs to figure out a realistic way to do it. It's no help to
6   say she's going to quit school and run away. She needs to
7   know how she can support herself.
8   PATTY: School can be a means to an end. Get her diploma
9   because it will allow her more options.
10   BOB: Exactly. If she graduates, it will be easier to find a job
11   in a different town.
12   LEADER: What advice do you have for Jill? Three specific
13   things?
14   PATTY: Vow not to complain about anything.
15   KEVIN: Pretend to like school.
16   BOB: Make a two-year plan. Figure out some ways to get the
17   life she wants.
18   LEADER: Will the first two people with problems please come
19   back? *(BONNIE and ROGER return. JILL stands. These three*
20   *face the others.)* You have heard suggested solutions to your
21   problems. Each of you agreed to choose at least one of
22   these suggestions and try it. What is your choice?
23   BONNIE: It makes sense for me to exercise after school in-
24   stead of eating. I'll do that.
25   ROGER: I've always thought it would be fun to be a clown,
26   but I never had the nerve to try it. I'm going to learn how
27   and then take my clown act to visit Children's Hospital.
28   *(All look at JILL. She stands defensively, arms crossed.)*
29   LEADER: Jill? Which suggestion do you accept?
30   JILL: You guys are weird, do you know that? Sitting around
31   like a bunch of amateur psychiatrists, picking apart other
32   people's problems. It's sick.
33   LEADER: You agreed to try at least one piece of advice. Which
34   one do you choose?
35   JILL: Nobody can make me do this. Once I leave this room,

1   you can't control what I do.
2   LEADER: Are you saying you want to back out of your
3   promise?
4   JILL: I'm saying your so-called suggestions are no good.
5   PATTY: How do you know until you try them?
6   JILL: Oh, sure. It's easy for you, isn't it? You who never had
7   a problem in your entire life can sit there and tell me to
8   change my attitude.
9   LEADER: Each of the people on this committee was chosen
10   because they have successfully overcome a serious prob-
11   lem of their own.
12   JILL: Oh, yeah? Like deciding what to wear to the dance?
13   You think there are easy answers to what's wrong in my
14   life. Well, you don't know what you're talking about. Just
15   because everything's rosy in your life, you think it can be
16   that way for me, too. All I have to do is smile and pretend
17   to be happy.
18   KEVIN: There have been some thorns in our roses, too.
19   LEADER: Jill, we aren't here to discuss their problems. We
20   want to know how you plan to help yourself solve your
21   problem.
22   PATTY: I don't mind telling her about my problem. Maybe it
23   will help. *(She stands and walks over to JILL.)* Two years
24   ago, my sister committed suicide. I found her when I went
25   home from school.
26   BOB: *(He stands and approaches JILL, too.)* My parents are al-
27   coholics. They've been in and out of more treatment pro-
28   grams than I can count. And I've been in and out of foster
29   homes since I was three years old.
30   KEVIN: *(Stands, too.)* I have defective kidneys. I've been on
31   dialysis for over a year. I'm hoping eventually to have a
32   kidney transplant, if a suitable donor can be found.
33   BONNIE: Wow! I didn't know all this.
34   LEADER: Thank you all for being so open. Jill, we are waiting
35   for your answer.

1   JILL: All right. So maybe I was wrong about you guys having
2   problems. But that doesn't change anything for me. I still
3   say school's a waste of time and this town is out of the
4   last century.
5   LEADER: Our time is up. Bonnie, Roger, and Jill, you may
6   leave.
7   JILL: Finally. *(She exits.)*
8   ROGER: Thanks for listening. I learned something about
9   myself.
10 BONNIE: Me, too. And I'm going to try really hard to lose
11   some weight. *(ROGER and BONNIE exit.)*
12 PATTY: Two out of three. I guess that isn't too bad.
13 KEVIN: I hope Jill doesn't run away. *(All start to exit.)*
14 BOB: I wonder what else we could have said to her.
15 LEADER: You did your best. Nobody can help Jill if she isn't
16   willing to help herself.
17
18
19
20
21
22
23
24
25
26
27
28
29
30
31
32
33
34
35

48

JUST A JOB

1   *CAST:* Three players, either sex: PERSON ONE, TWO and
2   THREE.
3   *(Directions: Speak the lines rapidly, in sing-song fashion: da-da-*
4   *dum, da-da-dum, da-da-da-da-da-da-dum, with no break in the*
5   *rhythm between speakers. Optional: Snap fingers on the accented*
6   *syllables.)*
7
8   **PERSON ONE:**   Just a job, just a job. All I need is just a job.
9   **Any job, any job. I'll work hard for extra cash.**
10   **PERSON TWO:**   Just a job, just a job. This girl really needs a
11   **job.**
12   **PERSON ONE:**   I'd work hard, I'd work hard, if I only had a
13   **job.**
14   **PERSON TWO:**   Just a job, just a job. This girl really needs a
15   **job.**
16   **PERSON ONE:**   I'll be prompt, every day, and I'll never phone
17   **in sick.**
18   **PERSON TWO:**   She'll work hard, she'll work hard. This girl
19   **really needs a job.**
20   **PERSON THREE:**   Can you type? Can you file? Have you any
21   **special skill?**
22   **PERSON ONE:**   I am smart; I am strong. I can work on Satur-
23   **day.**
24   **PERSON TWO:**   Try her out, tell her yes. Take a chance on
25   **someone young.**
26   **PERSON THREE:**   Can you cook? Can you add? Can you make
27   **the proper change?**
28   **PERSON: ONE:**   All my friends will be green. They'll wish they
29   **had found a job.**
30   **PERSON TWO:**   Sign her up, take her on. Give this girl a
31   **chance to work.**
32   **PERSON THREE:**   Any training? Any skills? Have you ever
33   **worked before?**

1	PERSON ONE: Just a job, any job. I'll work hard to earn
2	some cash.
3	PERSON TWO: She'll work hard, she'll work hard. Won't you
4	give this girl a job?
5	PERSON THREE: Can you saw? Drive a nail? Check the oil
6	in a car?
7	PERSON ONE: I can learn, I'll work hard. And I'll never, ever
8	quit.
9	PERSON TWO: Just a job, just a job. Won't you give this girl
10	a job?
11	PERSON THREE: Are you sure? Do you know? Do you know
12	how hard it is?
13	PERSON ONE: Need the cash, need the cash. Need a job to
14	buy a car.
15	PERSON TWO: Just a job, just a job. Won't you give this girl
16	a job?
17	PERSON THREE: Every day, every day. You must show up
18	every day.
19	PERSON ONE: I'll be there, without fail. I'll do anything you
20	say.
21	PERSON TWO: She'll work hard. She'll stay late. She'll do
22	anything you say.
23	PERSON THREE: No diploma and no skills. No experience
24	on a job.
25	PERSON ONE: Something fun, something wild. Nothing bor-
26	ing, nothing hard.
27	PERSON TWO: Just a job, just a job. All she wants is just a job.
28	PERSON THREE: After school, every day. It will take up all
29	your time.
30	PERSON ONE: Want a job, want a job. Something daring,
31	something bold.
32	PERSON TWO: Just a job, just a job. This girl really needs a
33	job.
34	PERSON ONE: Pay my bills, pay my bills. Need the cash to
35	pay my bills.

1   PERSON TWO: Need a job, any job. Can you give this girl a
2   chance?
3   PERSON THREE: There's one job you could do. Fry some
4   burgers, make some shakes.
5   PERSON TWO: Do you hear? This is great! You are going to
6   get a job!
7   PERSON ONE: Frying burgers? Making shakes? Not exactly
8   what I want.
9   PERSON THREE: It's a job, it's a job. It's a way to get a start.
10   PERSON ONE: Lousy pay, no prestige. I'll hold out for some-
11   thing else.
12   PERSON TWO: This girl's smart. She is bright. She deserves
13   a better job.
14   PERSON ONE: Want a job, want a job. Something worthy of
15   my time.
16   PERSON TWO: Of her time, of her time. Something worthy
17   of her time.
18   PERSON ONE: Buy a car, learn to ski. Get a TV of my own.
19   PERSON TWO: Just a job, just a job. All she wants is just a job.
20   PERSON ONE: Something different, something grand. Noth-
21   ing ordinary, please.
22   PERSON TWO: Just a job, just a job. Something worthy of
23   her time.
24   PERSON ONE: Nothing boring, nothing hard. But I really
25   want a job.
26   PERSON TWO: Just a job, just a job. All she wants is just a job.
27   PERSON ONE: With good pay, lots of pay. I deserve a lot of
28   pay.
29   PERSON TWO: Something fun, something wild. Nothing bor-
30   ing, nothing hard.
31   PERSON ONE: Just a job, just a job. All I want is just a job.
32   PERSON THREE: No diploma, no degree. She has never had
33   a job.
34   PERSON ONE: Lots of pay, lots of pay. I deserve a lot of pay.
35   PERSON TWO: Just a job, just a job. All she wants is just a job.

1   PERSON THREE: Sorry, kid. No experience. I don't have a
2   job for you.
3   PERSON TWO: No experience, no experience. All they say is,
4   "No experience."
5   PERSON ONE: Earn some cash, buy a car. Get some jingle
6   in my jeans.
7   PERSON TWO: She'd work hard, be on time. She deserves to
8   have a job.
9   PERSON THREE: Someone else has applied. I will give that
10   man a job.
11   PERSON ONE: Is he smart? Is he strong? Does he really need
12   the cash?
13   PERSON THREE: I don't know; I don't care. He'll fry burgers;
14   he'll make shakes.
15   PERSON TWO: There's no chance. You're too young. He
16   won't listen to a kid.
17   PERSON ONE: It's not fair. I'd work hard, if I only had a job.
18   PERSON TWO: Something fun, something wild. Nothing bor-
19   ing, nothing hard.
20   PERSON ONE: *(More slowly)* Just a job, just a job. All I want
21   is just a job.
22   ONE AND TWO TOGETHER: Just a job, just a job. It's so
23   hard to find a job.
24
25
26
27
28
29
30
31
32
33
34
35

49

A BABY OF MY OWN

1 *CAST:* Three players: BETTY, JILL, ROBYN.
2 *PROPS:* Doll wrapped in blanket. Gift-wrapped package contain-
3 ing something for a baby. Rocking chair, if possible. BETTY
4 wears a bathrobe. JILL and ROBYN wear casual clothes.
5 *SETTING:* BETTY's living room. Playlet can be done with three
6 plain chairs (or two chairs plus the rocker) for the set.
7 *AT RISE:* BETTY is On Stage, Left, holding the doll. If rocking
8 chair is used, she is rocking her baby.
9 *(JILL and ROBYN enter, Right, and walk slowly toward*
10 *BETTY. ROBYN carries the gift.)*
11
12 JILL: I can't wait to see him.
13 ROBYN: I've never seen a newborn baby before.
14 JILL: It's hard to imagine Betty as a mother. She is so lucky.
15 ROBYN: I don't know how lucky it is to have a baby when
16 you're sixteen years old and not married. I have a feeling
17 Betty wishes she'd been more careful.
18 JILL: I'd love to have a little baby of my own.
19 ROBYN: You would?
20 JILL: A sweet, little, cuddly baby that was all mine; someone
21 who would love me better than anyone in the whole world.
22 Wouldn't you like that?
23 ROBYN: Some day I'd like a baby, but not yet. *(They stop a*
24 *short distance from BETTY.)*
25 JILL: We came to see your baby.
26 ROBYN: And you. *(JILL and ROBYN stand next to BETTY to*
27 *admire baby.)*
28 JILL: Oh, isn't he sweet?
29 ROBYN: He's so little.
30 BETTY: Seven pounds, three ounces. He's gained back what
31 he lost after he was born.
32 JILL: He's adorable. He's the cutest thing I've ever seen.
33 BETTY: Do you want to hold him?

1   JILL: Oh, yes. *(BETTY carefully transfers doll to JILL. JILL and*
2   *ROBYN sit in other two chairs.)*
3   ROBYN: We brought you a little gift for Matthew. *(She hands*
4   *the package to BETTY.)*
5   BETTY: Thanks. That's really nice of you. *(She opens package*
6   *and removes gift.)*
7   JILL: We had a blast shopping for it. I never saw so many
8   darling little outfits.
9   BETTY: This is really nice. Thank you.
10 ROBYN: I hope it's something you need. We weren't sure what
11   you had.
12 BETTY: You couldn't guess wrong. I need everything.
13 JILL: I wanted to get some little high-top tennis shoes, but
14   Robyn talked me into being more practical.
15 ROBYN: How are you feeling?
16 BETTY: Tired. Matthew eats every three hours, so I don't get
17   much sleep.
18 JILL: Look at his tiny, little fingers.
19 ROBYN: Will you be coming back to school?
20 BETTY: Not this year. I want to but I have to find a job, and
21   right now I don't have anyone to watch Matthew.
22 ROBYN: What about your Mom?
23 BETTY: She works three days a week. Even if she didn't, I
24   couldn't leave Matthew with her all the time.
25 JILL: Why not? Most grandmothers love to babysit.
26 ROBYN: Not every day.
27 BETTY: Mom loves Matthew, but she says she raised her kids
28   and I can raise mine.
29 JILL: Well, if I had a baby, I'd rather stay home and take care
30   of him than go to school.
31 BETTY: Next year I hope I can go to school in the morning,
32   be with Matthew in the afternoon and evening, and then
33   work a night shift. He could be in daycare in the morning,
34   and Mom would babysit at night, when he'd be asleep the
35   whole time.

1   ROBYN: When would you sleep?
2   BETTY: Good question. *(JILL makes cooing noises and nuzzles*
3   *the doll.)*
4   ROBYN: Has Ben seen him?
5   BETTY: Once. He came to the hospital when Matthew was
6   born. He feels so guilty that I'm trapped at home and he's
7   still in school. His parents paid part of the hospital bill.
8   JILL: We thought you and Ben might get married.
9   BETTY: Neither of us wanted that. We aren't ready to get
10   married.
11   JILL: I am. All I need is a husband.
12   BETTY: Ben had to drop basketball.
13   JILL: He can't! He's the best center we have.
14   BETTY: He works after school now. He had to get a part-time
15   job, to help with Matthew's expenses.
16   ROBYN: I'm glad he's taking some responsibility.
17   JILL: Glad! How can you be glad? This means we probably
18   won't have a chance to go to the district playoffs this year.
19   Remember how much fun we had last year? Remember
20   the pep rally where the three of us did that silly skit?
21   ROBYN: We laughed so hard we couldn't even finish our act.
22   BETTY: That seems a hundred years ago, like a different
23   lifetime.
24   ROBYN: We'd better be going. *(She stands. JILL gives baby back*
25   *to BETTY.)*
26   BETTY: It was great to see you. And thanks for the present.
27   JILL: The whole gang is going out for pizza tomorrow night.
28   Why don't you come with us? You could bring Matthew
29   along, if you don't have anyone to watch him.
30   BETTY: *(Shakes her head no.)* I'm not ready for that. I can't fit
31   into any of my clothes. Thanks, anyway. And thanks for
32   coming over.
33   ROBYN: Good-by. *(JILL and ROBYN walk away. BETTY rocks*
34   *baby.)*
35   JILL: Did you ever see anything so adorable? Betty is so lucky.

1   ROBYN: I wouldn't trade places with her.
2   JILL: Well, I would. It would be wonderful to have a tiny,
3   little baby to love and take care of. A sweet, little baby,
4   all my own.
5
6
7
8
9
10
11
12
13
14
15
16
17
18
19
20
21
22
23
24
25
26
27
28
29
30
31
32
33
34
35

THE INHERITANCE

1   *CAST:*   Five players, two male, three female: SHARON, AMY,
2   MARK, ERIK, MS. BISHOP.
3   *SETTING:*   Scene is waiting room at attorney's office.
4   *(SHARON and AMY are On Stage at start.)*
5
6   SHARON: I can hardly wait to find out what Grandma left
7   us. For all we know, we might be rich.
8   AMY: I doubt that. She probably left her house and her money
9   to Dad and Uncle Jack. We'll probably each get something
10   personal, like a piece of jewelry.
11   SHARON: I hope I get her diamond earrings. Or is that what
12   you were hoping for?
13   AMY: *(Shakes her head)* I'm hoping I might get Freddy the
14   Teddy.
15   SHARON: That scruffy old teddy bear?
16   AMY: It was Grandma's when she was little. It's the only toy
17   that she had when she was small.
18   SHARON: All the fur is rubbed off, and he's missing an eye.
19   AMY: I don't care. Grandma loved Freddy the Teddy. Ever
20   since I can remember, he sat on her bed, right on the
21   pillow. She used to let me sleep with him when I was sick.
22   SHARON: I wonder why she never got a new eye for him.
23   AMY: I asked her that once. She said it's expensive to have
24   a quality restoration done on an antique toy, and she didn't
25   want to spend the money.
26   SHARON: I don't blame her. Well, you can have the bear; I'd
27   rather have something useful. And valuable. *(Enter MARK*
28   *and ERIK)*
29   MARK: Hi, cousins. Ready for the big reading of the will?
30   ERIK: If Grandma left me a bundle of money, I know exactly
31   what I'm going to spend it on. It's red, and it has four
32   wheels and a convertible top, and it drives like a dream.
33   SHARON: Well, I hope you didn't sign any papers yet. Maybe

1   all you'll get is a set of dishes.

2   MARK: Grandma wouldn't do that to us.

3   AMY: I think we should quit talking about what we hope she

4   left us. It sounds greedy.

5   ERIK: What do most people talk about while they're waiting

6   to hear the terms of someone's will?

7   MARK: *(Points Off Stage)* **What's going on in there? We thought**

8   we were late.

9   SHARON: The attorney is still talking to our dad and yours.

10   When she's through with them, she'll come out and talk

11   to us.

12   ERIK: I could hardly sleep last night. I kept thinking about

13   that little red car with the big engine. *(MS. BISHOP enters,*

14   *carrying briefcase or file folder. All stand.)*

15   BISHOP: Good afternoon. I'm Alison Bishop, your grand-

16   mother's attorney.

17   SHARON: I'm Sharon Hamilton. This is my sister, Amy, and

18   my cousins, Mark and Erik. *(All shake hands.)*

19   BISHOP: Please sit down. *(They do.)* This won't take long.

20   Your grandmother left most of her estate to her two sons,

21   your fathers, to be evenly divided between them. She also

22   left the following to her grandchildren: *(She reads from will.)*

23   To Mark: The pocket watch that belonged to her husband.

24   MARK: Oh! Grandpa's watch. I'd forgotten about that. He

25   taught me to tell time on it.

26   BISHOP: To Sharon: Her diamond earrings. *(SHARON grins*

27   *broadly, looks at AMY and nods.)* To Erik: Her collection of

28   bird books.

29   ERIK: No kidding. The bird books! She and I used to watch

30   the birds at the bird feeder, and we made a little X in the

31   books whenever we identified one.

32   BISHOP: To Amy: Freddy the Teddy. *(AMY bursts into tears.)*

33   MARK: Maybe you can sell him. Some of those old toys are

34   worth money.

35   SHARON: That isn't why she's crying. She wanted the bear.

1   ERIK: She did? Why?

2   MARK: Even though it isn't a bundle of cash, I'm glad I got

3   Grandpa's watch.

4   BISHOP: There's something more. Your grandmother loved

5   to keep in touch with all of you. For the last six years,

6   whenever one of you called her on the phone, or stopped

7   to visit, she put ten dollars in a special savings account in

8   your name. She even put ten dollars in if you wrote a

9   thank-you letter when she gave you a gift.

10   MARK: I always wrote "thanks" on the back of the check

11   when I signed it. I hope she saw that.

12   BISHOP: There were four accounts, one for each of you, and

13   instructions for distributing the money. She kept careful

14   records and she said to tell you this is her way of thanking

15   you for letting her share your lives. *(She hands each of them*

16   *a check. AMY stares at hers during next five speeches.)*

17   SHARON: Mine's for two hundred, fifty-two dollars and four

18   cents. What's yours?

19   MARK: Ninty-nine dollars and thirty-two cents. I guess she

20   didn't look at the back of her cancelled checks.

21   ERIK: Mine's almost five hundred dollars! Four-eighty-nine

22   and thirteen cents. I didn't realize I called Grandma that

23   often.

24   BISHOP: That includes interest.

25   MARK: What about yours, Amy? I hope you got something

26   besides that worn-out, old bear.

27   SHARON: You were always calling Grandma and going over

28   there. *(AMY nods yes.)* Well, how much did you get? *(AMY*

29   *is still emotional and can't talk. She hands her check to SHAR-*

30   *ON.)* Wow!

31   ERIK: How much?

32   SHARON: Fifteen thousand, six hundred eighty-three dollars

33   and two cents.

34   ERIK: Fifteen thousand dollars?

35   MARK: It was pretty sneaky of Grandma not to tell us she

```
1          was doing this.
2    BISHOP:  It wouldn't have been the same if you had known.
3          She would have thought you called her because of the
4          money.
5    AMY:  I called Grandma and went over because I loved her.
6          I didn't expect anything like this.
7    ERIK:  I don't suppose you'd like to buy a sweet, little, red car
8          and lend it to your favorite cousin?
9    AMY:  Sorry.
10   ERIK:  I didn't think so.
11   SHARON:  Practical Amy will save it all for college. Right?
12   AMY:  Most of it, but not all. I'm going to spend some right
13          away.
14   MARK:  Shopping mall, here she comes.
15   AMY:  Not the mall. The phone book. I need to find someone
16          who does restoration work on antique toys. Freddy the
17          Teddy is going to have a new glass eye.
18   SHARON:  It's about time.
19   AMY:  And then he'll have a special place on my bed. Right
20          on the pillow.
21
22
23
24
25
26
27
28
29
30
31
32
33
34
35
```

51

SOMEBODY SHOULD
DO SOMETHING

1   CAST: Four players: RITA, TIM, KAY, NICKY.
2   *(RITA is On Stage at start. TIM enters.)*
3
4   RITA: Hi, Tim. Where are you going?
5   TIM: To the school office. This is the last day to sign up for
6   litter duty.
7   RITA: The parking lot and school yard sure look better since
8   that litter program started. There used to be paper blowing
9   all over the place. Somebody should have done something
10   about it years ago.
11   TIM: It's making people more careful, too. The first time I
12   worked on litter pickup, we filled twenty bags with trash.
13   Last time, we only filled four bags, and we did the whole
14   neighborhood, not just the school.
15   RITA: How often does somebody do the litter pickup?
16   TIM: One Saturday morning every month. Haven't you had
17   a turn? I thought everyone was working once each quar-
18   ter.
19   RITA: I—uh, haven't had a chance to sign up yet.
20   TIM: Come and sign up with me now. Maybe we could work
21   the same shift.
22   RITA: My schedule is pretty busy.
23   TIM: So is mine. *(RITA exits. KAY enters.)* Hi Kay. What's the
24   matter? You look upset.
25   KAY: I am upset. I just saw a little kid almost get hit trying
26   to cross the street. He was in the crosswalk, too, but the
27   car didn't even slow down. Somebody should do some-
28   thing about the traffic outside the school. We need a traffic
29   light.
30   TIM: Maybe we could have everyone sign a petition and give
31   it to the city council. Maybe they don't know how bad the
32   situation is.
33   KAY: The city council won't pay any attention to a bunch of

1	teenagers. Besides, traffic lights cost a fortune.
2	TIM: Maybe we could organize crossing guards, with flags.
3	Lots of kids from the elementary school walk by here every
4	day. If we older kids took turns being the guards, it
5	wouldn't cost the school anything except the money to
6	buy the red flags.
7	KAY: That's a good idea. Somebody should do that.
8	TIM: I could come early one day every week, to help. I bet
9	lots of kids would be willing to do it. Let's ask the principal
10	to meet with us and see if we can get it started.
11	KAY: I can't come early because my dad drops me off every
12	day on his way to work.
13	TIM: Oh. Well, what about after school? We would need cross-
14	ing guards then, too.
15	KAY: My mom picks me up on her way home. In fact, there
16	she is now. See you later. *(KAY exits. NICKY enters.)*
17	NICKY: Have you heard about the Blast Mr. Ryan party?
18	TIM: You mean someone's having a retirement party for Mr.
19	Ryan?
20	NICKY: Not exactly. It's a celebration party because he's re-
21	tiring, but he won't be invited. Everyone's going to bring
22	food and tell why they're glad they'll never have Mr. Ryan
23	for English again. They're going to write all the comments
24	in a notebook and leave it on Mr. Ryan's desk.
25	TIM: That's mean. I like Mr. Ryan.
26	NICKY: Me, too. I thought he was a pretty good teacher. But
27	you know how ideas like that can get out of hand.
28	TIM: Who started it?
29	NICKY: I don't know. Shelly told me about it, and she said
30	Matthew told her.
31	TIM: Are they going to go?
32	NICKY: I guess so.
33	TIM: Well, I'm not.
34	NICKY: Good. Then I won't go, either.
35	TIM: I think we should tell Mr. Ryan what's going on.

1   NICKY: Are you nuts? Why should we get blamed when we
2   didn't have anything to do with it?
3   TIM: If we told him, he wouldn't blame us, and he might be
4   able to put a stop to it.
5   NICKY: You can tell him if you want to, but I'm not having
6   anything to do with it. He'll be furious.
7   TIM: Think how badly his feelings will be hurt if the party
8   takes place. He's taught here for a long time. His last week
9   shouldn't be spoiled by a mean trick like that. It isn't right.
10 NICKY: I told Shelly that. I said somebody should put a stop
11   to it.
12 TIM: I'm going to tell one of the other teachers. Right now.
13   They'll know what to do. Maybe they can step in and pre-
14   vent the whole thing from happening. Maybe Mr. Ryan
15   won't ever have to know anything about it.
16 NICKY: Why are you sticking your neck out? You never even
17   had Mr. Ryan, did you?
18 TIM: No. But the Blast Mr. Ryan party is wrong, and some-
19   body ought to stop it.
20 NICKY: I agree, but . . .
21 TIM: I am somebody. *(TIM exits one direction. NICKY shrugs*
22   *and exits the other direction.)*
23
24
25
26
27
28
29
30
31
32
33
34
35

52

TRANSFORMATION

1   *CAST:*   Three female students, two male students: LISA, JANE,
2   WENDY, ROY, BARRY. TEACHER, either sex.
3   *SETTING:*   Set is bare except for five plain chairs in semi-circle,
4   facing the audience.
5   *(LISA and JANE enter, talking as they enter.)*
6

7   LISA: Are you ready for this?
8   JANE: I guess so.
9   LISA: You were smart to choose dog. That's an easy one. I
10   decided to be an elephant. My dad had to drive me to the
11   library last night. *(ROY enters. LISA and JANE sit in two*
12   *center chairs.)*
13   ROY: Hi.
14   LISA: Hi, Roy. Did you choose an animal?
15   ROY: Can you believe this? I've heard of some weird assign-
16   ments, but I've never been told to think like a pig before.
17   *(ROY sits next to LISA.)*
18   JANE: You're going to be a pig? Oh, that's great. Did you
19   practice oinking?
20   ROY: No, I practiced eating.
21   LISA: At least this class is never boring. *(WENDY enters. Others*
22   *ignore her. She hesitates, as if wondering where to sit. BARRY*
23   *enters. He comes up behind WENDY.)*
24   BARRY: Out of my way, stupid.
25   WENDY: Sorry. *(She moves aside. BARRY moves, too, and stays*
26   *directly behind her.)*
27   BARRY: I said, get out of my way. *(He punches her lightly—not*
28   *hard enough to hurt, but she jumps nervously.)*
29   LISA: Leave her alone, Barry.
30   BARRY: *(Mimicking)* Leave her alone, Barry. Poor little thing
31   can't defend herself. *(WENDY sidles to closest chair, on end*
32   *of semicircle, and sits down. BARRY promptly stands in front*
33   *of her.)* Can't you read?

1 WENDY: What?
2 BARRY: Can't you read? That's my chair. There's a sign right
3   on the seat that says so. *(LISA, JANE and ROY snicker.)*
4 WENDY: I didn't see any sign.
5 BARRY: Well, you'd better stand up and look again. *(WENDY*
6   *stands. There is no sign. BARRY sits in the chair. Others laugh.)*
7   Thank you very much. *(WENDY crosses to opposite end chair*
8   *and sits down. TEACHER enters and stands slightly to side of*
9   *chairs, where she can face students and audience.)*
10 TEACHER: Good morning.
11 ALL EXCEPT WENDY: Good morning.
12 TEACHER: I trust each of you has given some thought to
13   becoming an animal for today. *(BARRY makes his hands*
14   *into claws, bares his teeth and growls.)*
15 LISA: Barry's already an animal.
16 ROY: That's right. Maybe he'll get a passing grade, for a
17   change.
18 TEACHER: For a brief time during today's class, each of you
19   will become, in your mind, some other form of life. You
20   will mentally assume that life form and then share that
21   species' feelings about us humans. I hope you gave this
22   assignment some serious thought since yesterday. Who
23   has decided which animal they want to be?
24 BARRY: I have. I'll be a party animal. *(He moves his arms, as*
25   *if dancing.)*
26 TEACHER: As I told you, it's also permissible to be a tree or
27   a bird or a fish.
28 BARRY: Wendy's a worm. And I'm going fishing.
29 TEACHER: Has anyone chosen a life form for this project?
30   If not, I will assign the roles.
31 LISA: I decided to be an elephant.
32 BARRY: I *told* you if you kept eating so much junk food, you'd
33   get fat, but I didn't think you'd get *that* fat.
34 TEACHER: Barry, please be quiet until you're called on. Did
35   anyone else select an animal?

1   JANE: I did. I'm going to be a dog.

2   ROY: I'm going to be a pig.

3   BARRY: Me, too. Where's the food? I didn't have any break-

4   fast.

5   TEACHER: Wendy, did you choose an animal? *(WENDY nods*

6   *her head yes.)* Did you pick the caterpillar, as I suggested?

7   *(WENDY nods yes.)* Good. Then you are a caterpillar.

8   BARRY: And I have a big, heavy foot that's going to squash

9   you.

10   TEACHER: That's enough, Barry. You are a deer.

11   BARRY: I know I'm a dear. Dear Barry. Dear, sweet Barry.

12   TEACHER: D-e-e-r.

13   LISA: As in Bambi.

14   TEACHER: You will each have one minute to tell how you

15   feel. Tell what makes you happy and what frightens you.

16   Remember always to talk as if you were the animal you've

17   been assigned. As you speak, I may ask a question now

18   and then, to help you think through your feelings. For the

19   purposes of this exercise, I am the voice of the wind. I am

20   unseen, but each of you can hear me, and you understand

21   in your own language.

22   BARRY: *(Stage whisper)* I always said she was long-winded.

23   LISA: Shut up, Barry. This sounds like fun, and you're spoil-

24   ing it.

25   TEACHER: Everyone else must be silent while each animal

26   speaks. I'm serious about that, Barry. Any comments and

27   you're out of here, as in suspended.

28   BARRY: OK, OK. Nobody can take a joke.

29   TEACHER: Lisa, we'll begin with you. Please stand and close

30   your eyes. *(LISA stands, eyes closed.)* You are now an

31   elephant. Please tell us how you feel.

32   LISA: I'm huge. When I walk through the jungle, I crush

33   plants and bushes under my big feet. It's hot here. It is

34   the dry season, and I am thirsty. I see a young elephant,

35   and I remember how it was to be smaller.

1   TEACHER: What do you like to do best, elephant?

2   LISA: I like to be with my family. Twice a year, in the rainy

3   season, my group travels and feeds near other groups,

4   and it is wonderful to see these friends again. We dance

5   and rub against each other. We click our tusks and entwine

6   our trunks. They are just as happy to see me as I am to

7   see them.

8   TEACHER: And what do you like least about your life?

9   LISA: The poachers who kill us to get our ivory tusks. It is

10   such a waste of life. Our tusks keep growing throughout

11   our lifetime; if the hunters would allow us to die of old

12   age, they would have far more ivory to sell—many hundred

13   pounds, rather than only ten or twenty. I see the bones of

14   my former friends who did not escape the poachers. Soon,

15   I fear, there will be no friends. There will be no family.

16   There will be no elephants.

17   TEACHER: Thank you, elephant. You may sit down now.

18   *(LISA sits.)* Next we'll hear from the pig. *(ROY stands.)* Eyes

19   closed, please. *(He does.)* How does it feel to be a pig?

20   ROY: I like to roll in the mud. There's a big, black mudhole

21   in my pigpen, and I go there when it's hot. It gets the flies

22   off my skin. It's hard to be so fat, though. I can't move

23   fast, and my legs get tired, so I have to rest a lot. But I am

24   intelligent. The other pigs and I are just as smart as dogs.

25   *(Pause)*

26   TEACHER: You are leaving your pen. You are put on a truck

27   with other pigs and taken to a slaughter house. How do

28   you feel now?

29   ROY: I'm scared. I can't keep my balance on the truck. All

30   the pigs are squealing and rocking back and forth. I feel

31   sick, and I want to go back to my pen and lie in my mud-

32   hole, but I can't. *(His voice rises as he gets into the pig role.)*

33   I can't get out of this damn truck. Let me out!

34   TEACHER: The truck has stopped now. *(Slight pause)*

35   ROY: *(Voice lower again, but it rises dramatically during this speech.)*

1   I'm in a place with the other pigs, but I don't like it. We're
2   crowded. Now some people come. One at a time, they push
3   us along a ramp. They poke me with a stick, to make me
4   move. It smells bad here. I hear other pigs screaming. They
5   are afraid. I am afraid, too. I don't know why I'm here or
6   what is happening. I see the pigs in front of me on the
7   ramp. A man sticks one of them with a long knife. The pig
8   screams. Blood gushes. *(WENDY covers her ears, unable to*
9   *listen.)* I try to turn back. I can't. I have to go forward.
10   Now the pig in front of me is stuck with the knife. It is my
11   turn next. I see the knife. I can't get away. I scream and
12   struggle. Why? Why?!
13 TEACHER: Stop there, pig. Open your eyes. *(ROY opens eyes.*
14   *He appears shaken. LISA and JANE are on the verge of tears.)*
15   Thank you, Roy. You may sit down now. Jane, please stand
16   and tell us how it feels to be a dog.
17 JANE: Most of the time I like being a dog. It's fun when my
18   owner pets me and plays with me. I like to chase my ball,
19   and I like to roll in the grass and scratch my back. But
20   sometimes I get very hungry, and my owner doesn't come
21   home to feed me on time. And sometimes, when he's angry,
22   he hits me with a newspaper and yells at me, and I don't
23   understand why. All I want is to be a good dog and get
24   food and love.
25 TEACHER: What is the worst part about your life, dog?
26 JANE: I hate it when my owner puts a doggie treat on top of
27   my nose and then says "no, no," and won't let me eat it.
28   It smells so good and my stomach grumbles, but he keeps
29   saying "no," and if I take the treat, he spanks me. I don't
30   understand why he gets the treat out if he doesn't want
31   me to have it. He never eats doggie treats, so I know he
32   doesn't want it himself. Just once, I wish he would give
33   one to me as a gift, without making me balance it on my
34   nose first.
35 TEACHER: Thank you, dog. You may sit down now.

1   BARRY: Sit. Stay.
2   TEACHER: *(Warning)* **Barry** . . . *(BARRY clamps hand over his*
3   *mouth.)* **Since you are so anxious to talk, let's hear what**
4   **the deer has to say.** *(BARRY stands and closes his eyes. He*
5   *says nothing for a couple of seconds.)* **Deer, do you like how**
6   **you look?**
7   BARRY: Yeah. Yeah. I'm a good-looking buck, with antlers.
8   A big, strong buck.
9   TEACHER: Can you run fast?
10   BARRY: I can run fast. And jump. I can jump over fences like
11   they were nothing.
12   TEACHER: Where do you live?
13   BARRY: In the forest, with the other deer. We eat the leaves
14   off the trees, I think.
15   TEACHER: How do you feel during hunting season?
16   BARRY: Huh?
17   TEACHER: Pretend it is hunting season. There are hunters
18   in the forest trying to find you and the other deer.
19   BARRY: I run away when I smell the humans. I can run faster
20   than they can.
21   TEACHER: No matter which way you run, there are more
22   hunters. You hear shots. *(Pause, waiting for BARRY to speak.*
23   *He doesn't.)* **They shot your friend.**
24   BARRY: I ran away in time.
25   TEACHER: But they shot your friend. They have powerful
26   guns, and you have nothing. *(No answer)* **Do you hear the**
27   **footsteps of the hunters? They are all through your forest,**
28   **and none of the deer is safe.** *(Pause)* **How do you feel now?**
29   BARRY: *(With sudden intensity)* **I want to put my head down**
30   and ram the hunters with my antlers. I want to stamp on
31   them with my hooves. But they will shoot me if I start to
32   do that. All I can do is run and try to hide, and there is
33   no place to hide.
34   TEACHER: Thank you. You may open your eyes. *(BARRY*
35   *does, blinks, looks around as if he isn't sure where he is. He sits*

1   *down.)* **Wendy, it is time for you to be a caterpillar.**

2   **WENDY: Do I have to?**

3   **TEACHER: Just do what the others have done. Tell how it**

4   **feels to see life from the viewpoint of a caterpillar.** *(WENDY*

5   *rubs hands together nervously, takes a deep breath, closes eyes.*

6   *Says nothing.)* **Begin, please.**

7   **WENDY: All the other creatures are bigger than I am. They're**

8   **faster than I am. I creep carefully along a branch, fearful**

9   **that a bird will land and eat me. I slink slowly along the**

10   **sidewalk, expecting to be stomped on at any moment. It's**

11   **terrible always to be afraid. I am plain and ugly, and I**

12   **can't do anything clever like the other animals do.**

13   **TEACHER: You can build a cocoon. Enclose yourself in a**

14   **cocoon.**

15   **WENDY: *(Hunches over, hugging herself.)* I like it in my cocoon.**

16   **It is snug and safe here, and none of the others can find**

17   **me. I curl up tight and see only the inner walls, which look**

18   **like gossamer with the dim light filtering through. I wish**

19   **I could stay in this cocoon forever.**

20   **TEACHER: Life continues, Wendy. You are now becoming a**

21   **beautiful butterfly.**

22   **WENDY: *(During this speech, WENDY gradually stands tall,***

23   *shoulders back.)* **The cocoon falls away. I stretch and yawn.**

24   **As I move, I realize I am no longer a caterpillar. In as-**

25   **tonishment, I discover that I have wings: lovely, yellow**

26   **wings with blue and orange markings. I flutter them, ex-**

27   **perimenting to be sure they work. They do. I leave the**

28   **empty cocoon behind and fly to the top branch of an apple**

29   **tree. I move swiftly and surely through the air. No bird**

30   **will eat me now. I sit on the top of the tree, and I yell,**

31   **"Hey, world! Look at me! See what's happened? I'm not**

32   **an ugly caterpillar anymore. I'm a butterfly. A beautiful**

33   **butterfly!"**

34   **TEACHER: Have you changed in any other way, besides your**

35   **looks?**

1   WENDY: Oh, yes. I am free now. Free of fear. Free of self-
2   doubt. Free of that stifling cocoon that didn't allow me to
3   move. And now that I know how it feels, I won't ever be
4   anything but free again. *(LISA, JANE and ROY spontane-*
5   *ously applaud. WENDY opens her eyes in surprise. She looks at*
6   *the others, including BARRY. This is the first time in the skit*
7   *that she has made eye contact with anyone. She continues to*
8   *stand straight, with confidence.)*
9   TEACHER: You may sit down, Wendy. *(She does.)* Now that
10   you've heard some of the animals speak, does anyone want
11   to share how you felt during our earth image skit?
12   LISA: Ashamed. Humans act as if we're the only creatures
13   who have any rights.
14   ROY: I think I just became a vegetarian.
15   TEACHER: Remember that most meat packing companies
16   use hog immobilizers and other methods for minimizing
17   an animal's pain and terror.
18   ROY: It was scary on the truck, too.
19   TEACHER: How do you feel about the dog whose owner put
20   treats on his nose and made him wait to get them?
21   LISA: I saw my uncle do that with his dog once, and I felt
22   sorry for the poor dog. It seemed so mean and senseless.
23   ROY: Your uncle wanted to show his power.
24   JANE: He had the power not to get the treat out in the first
25   place.
26   TEACHER: Do you see any correlation between that dog
27   scene and the deer who was being hunted?
28   JANE: Power again, huh?
29   WENDY: It's terrible to be helpless. To not have any power.
30   *(The others are surprised to have WENDY volunteer an opinion.)*
31   The dog and the deer were both in that position.
32   LISA: So was the elephant.
33   ROY: So was the pig.
34   BARRY: Come on, you're putting human thoughts in the ani-
35   mals' heads. We don't know if the deer are really scared

1   of the hunters.

2 LISA: Oh, get serious. Of course they're scared. They run

3   away, don't they?

4 BARRY: Well, it's legal to hunt deer and it's legal to eat pork

5   chops and it's legal to train your dog any way you want.

6   I don't see what everybody's looking so guilty about. None

7   of us ever cut the tusks off an elephant.

8 WENDY: Just because something is legal doesn't mean it's

9   right. *(The others are astonished at this remark.)*

10 BARRY: What are you, a Supreme Court justice?

11 ROY: Can you honestly say that you could go home right now

12   and eat a pork chop?

13 BARRY: You bet I could. With applesauce on the side.

14 JANE: You're disgusting.

15 BARRY: Now, wait a minute. How many of you ate meat yes-

16   terday? *(No answer. They all look at each other.)* I rest my case.

17 TEACHER: The purpose of this class was not to make you

18   into vegetarians. It was to help you realize that we are not

19   the only inhabitants of our planet. Our attitudes and ac-

20   tions affect thousands of species besides our own.

21 LISA: No elephant should have to die so that some person

22   can have ivory cuff links.

23 TEACHER: What if there are people, living in poverty, who

24   kill elephants and sell the ivory in order to get money so

25   they have enough food?

26 JANE: There should be other ways to escape poverty.

27 LISA: It's still wrong to kill the elephants.

28 TEACHER: Our time is nearly up. *(BARRY raises fist in silent*

29   *cheer.)* Before we leave, each animal will offer a gift to us

30   humans.

31 JANE: It seems more like we owe them a present.

32 TEACHER: Roy, we'll start with you. What does the pig offer

33   us?

34 ROY: Tolerance. As pig, I knew fear, but not hatred.

35 JANE: Dog offers loyalty. Even when my master hit me and

1   forced me to balance my treat on my nose, I still loved
2   him. I remained loyal.
3   TEACHER: Elephant? What gift do you give us?
4   LISA: Stability. I have endured for thousands of years; I do
5   not change my ways.
6   TEACHER: Caterpillar?
7   WENDY: Caterpillar isn't here. Butterfly offers faith. If we
8   believe in our own inner beauty, we can change and be-
9   come that which we admire.
10   TEACHER: Deer? Do you have a gift for the humans?
11   BARRY: You bet I do. Venison steaks.
12   JANE: Why don't you grow up?
13   LISA: He can't. His mentality is stuck at age one.
14   BARRY: What's the matter with everybody? Why are you all
15   picking on me all of a sudden?
16   TEACHER: I hope you'll think about other life forms more
17   often because of today's class. Imagine the results of your
18   actions, and take responsibility for them. Care about all
19   of earth, not just yourself. Class is dismissed. *(TEACHER*
20   *exits. Others stand and start to leave.)*
21   LISA: That was pretty heavy stuff.
22   ROY: I was going to make a joke out of being a pig and then,
23   all of a sudden, I had this image of the slaughter house,
24   and it seemed so real. *(LISA, JANE and ROY all exit. As*
25   *WENDY walks off, BARRY goes up behind her and punches*
26   *her. She whirls around to face him.)*
27   WENDY: If you ever touch me again, I will report you to the
28   principal *and* to the police.
29   BARRY: Huh?
30   WENDY: You will get kicked out of school. I will charge you
31   with harassment. If I have to, I will take you to court.
32   BARRY: *(Puts hands up, as if in surrender)* OK, OK. I was only
33   kidding.
34   WENDY: In the future, keep your hands to yourself and stay
35   out of my way. *(WENDY marches decisively off.)*

1   **BARRY:** *(Dumbfounded, he watches her leave.)* **Some butterfly.**
2   *(He exits.)*
3
4
5
6
7
8
9
10
11
12
13
14
15
16
17
18
19
20
21
22
23
24
25
26
27
28
29
30
31
32
33
34
35

53

STANDARD ANSWERS

1   *CAST:*   One PARENT, four STUDENTS.

2   No setting necessary.

3   *AT RISE:*   The four STUDENTS are seated on the floor. PARENT,

4   standing, addresses the audience.

5

6   PARENT: I am Parent. I am Author. All other parents in the

7   universe use my book as their guide to raising children.

8   They use it now; they used it a hundred years ago; they

9   will use it in the future. It is timeless and ageless.

10   It is the best-kept secret ever. All parents know about

11   it; kids never know, until they grow up and become parents

12   themselves, and by then, they are ready to use my book

13   and so they willingly perpetuate the secret, keeping it

14   going throughout infinity.

15   What book? you ask. All right. I will share the secret,

16   even though some of you in the audience are not yet par-

17   ents yourselves. I am the author of *The Parents' Book of*

18   *Standard Answers.* You may have wondered why it is that

19   parents in New York City and parents in Taos, New

20   Mexico, will answer certain questions exactly the same

21   way. It is because they all use my book.

22   To demonstrate the remarkable universality of my

23   book, I have asked three students to assist me. *(Three STU-*

24   *DENTS stand.)* No matter what they say to me, my replies

25   will come from *The Parents' Book of Standard Answers.*

26   STUDENT ONE: I studied for that test. I don't know why I

27   failed it.

28   PARENT: You didn't study hard enough.

29   STUDENT TWO: I'm full.

30   PARENT: Eat your vegetables, or you don't get dessert.

31   STUDENT THREE: Why can't I go? Give me one good reason.

32   PARENT: Because I said so.

33   STUDENT ONE: It isn't fair.

1　PARENT:　Life isn't always fair.
2　STUDENT TWO:　All the other kids are doing it.
3　PARENT:　I don't care what the other kids do. You are not
4　　　the other kids.
5　STUDENT THREE:　Can I go now?
6　PARENT:　*May* I go now?
7　STUDENT ONE:　Can I take the car to school today?
8　PARENT:　What's wrong with the bus?
9　STUDENT TWO:　Can I take the car to school today?
10　PARENT:　When I was your age, I used to walk two miles to
11　　　school every day.
12　STUDENT THREE:　Don't you trust me?
13　PARENT:　I remember what I was like at your age.
14　STUDENT ONE:　Why do I have to clean my room? It just gets
15　　　dirty again.
16　PARENT:　If you don't clean your room, you'll have spider
17　　　nests in it.
18　STUDENT TWO:　I think I'll quit school and get a job.
19　PARENT:　You'll be sorry.
20　STUDENT THREE:　I want to make some money so I can buy
21　　　a car.
22　PARENT:　Something wrong with your legs?
23　STUDENT TWO:　Someday I'm leaving this hick town. I'll
24　　　travel all over the world.
25　PARENT:　There's no place like home.
26　STUDENT ONE:　You're mean.
27　PARENT:　It's for your own good.
28　STUDENT TWO:　Why can't I go? Give me one good reason.
29　PARENT:　Someday, when you're my age, you'll understand.
30　STUDENT THREE:　I didn't ask to be born.
31　PARENT:　Well, it's too late now.
32　STUDENT ONE:　There's nothing to eat around here.
33　PARENT:　Have an apple.
34　STUDENT TWO:　There's nothing to do around here.
35　PARENT:　Read a book.

1   STUDENT THREE: I'm bored.

2   PARENT: Mow the lawn. *(Fourth STUDENT leaps to his feet*

3   *and shouts:)*

4   STUDENT FOUR: I am Child. I am Author. I also wrote a

5   book that has been used for decades. Every child intui-

6   tively knows my book; it is part of the wisdom of the ages,

7   which is passed along on the wind. My book is *The Kids'*

8   *Book of Standard Answers.*

9   PARENT: What are you doing?

10   STUDENT FOUR: Nothing.

11   PARENT: Don't interrupt.

12   STUDENT FOUR: I'm not interrupting. I'm joining the con-

13   versation.

14   PARENT: We'll discuss this later.

15   STUDENT FOUR: I want to discuss it now.

16   PARENT: This isn't a good time for it.

17   STUDENT FOUR: Why not?

18   PARENT: Drink your milk.

19   STUDENT FOUR: I'm full.

20   PARENT: Who ate all the cookies?

21   STUDENT FOUR: Not me.

22   PARENT: Who tracked mud on the carpet?

23   STUDENT FOUR: I don't know.

24   PARENT: Did you hear what I said?

25   STUDENT FOUR: Huh?

26   PARENT: You kids are driving me crazy with your fighting.

27   STUDENT FOUR: He hit me first.

28   PARENT: You've been on the phone for forty-five minutes.

29   Someone may be trying to call.

30   STUDENT FOUR: Who?

31   PARENT: I don't know who, but it's time for you to hang up.

32   STUDENT FOUR: I'm not done talking.

33   PARENT: Brussels sprouts are good for you.

34   STUDENT FOUR: Yuck.

35   PARENT: This concludes our demonstration.

1   **STUDENT ONE:**   Wait a minute. I'm not finished.
2   **STUDENT TWO:**   Me, either. I want to say more.
3   **STUDENT THREE:**   Why do we have to stop now?
4   **PARENT:**   Because I said so. *(Four STUDENTS look at each*
5   *other, shrug helplessly, and exit, followed by PARENT.)*
6
7
8
9
10
11
12
13
14
15
16
17
18
19
20
21
22
23
24
25
26
27
28
29
30
31
32
33
34
35

INVISIBLE BOXES

1   *CAST:*   Three players: ANDREW, PHIL, WALLY.
2   *SETTING:*   School.
3   *(ANDREW is On Stage at start. PHIL enters.)*
4
5   PHIL: You are not going to believe this. Wally Humphrey was
6   in the box!
7   ANDREW: What box?
8   PHIL: The big cardboard box. The one Miss Winthrip got from
9   the appliance store, to use as a prop for the school play.
10   She was going to clean the stage and when she pushed
11   the box to move it, it wouldn't budge. Turns out Wally was
12   inside it.
13   ANDREW: Why?
14   PHIL: Good question. Why would anyone want to sit inside
15   an empty cardboard box?
16   ANDREW: I suppose so he wouldn't have to go to class. In
17   homeroom yesterday, Mr. Thomas asked Wally why he kept
18   cutting classes, and Wally said because school is boring.
19   PHIL: Sitting alone in a box isn't?
20   ANDREW: I wonder how he got in it. It must be six feet high.
21   PHIL: It was upside down, so all he had to do was lift up one
22   side and crawl under. Talk about weird! He practically
23   scared Miss Winthrip to death. She tipped the box over,
24   to see why it wouldn't move, and there was Wally.
25   ANDREW: It would be dark in the box. He couldn't read or
26   anything. How long was he in there?
27   PHIL: Since third period.
28   ANDREW: That's more than three hours! I wonder how long
29   he would have stayed if Miss Winthrip hadn't found him.
30   PHIL: He was probably going to hide there until school was
31   out and everyone had left and then vandalize the school.
32   ANDREW: It's sad, isn't it, that anyone would rather sit all
33   alone in an empty box than to attend class? He must really

1   hate school.

2 PHIL: You'd hate school, too, if you were flunking practically

3   every subject. Of course, it's his own fault. He cuts class

4   half the time, and he never does any assignments.

5 ANDREW: Does he have any friends?

6 PHIL: Not that I know of. He's a loner.

7 ANDREW: I wonder what his family is like. Maybe he has

8   problems at home.

9 PHIL: Lots of kids have problems at home; that doesn't mean

10   they drop out of society and shut themselves up in an

11   empty box.

12 ANDREW: Look. Wally's coming out of the principal's office

13   right now. I'm going to ask him why he did it.

14 PHIL: I wouldn't do that. He might get mad.

15 ANDREW: Why would he get mad? I'm just curious. *(WALLY*

16   *enters. When he sees ANDREW and PHIL, he tries to avoid them.*

17   *ANDREW goes up to WALLY.)* I hear you were hiding in

18   that big box. *(WALLY keeps walking.)* What was it like inside?

19   Could you hear anything?

20 WALLY: *(Stops)* What's it to you?

21 ANDREW: It sounds like fun. I wish I'd thought of doing that.

22 PHIL: You do?

23 ANDREW: It was a good joke on Miss Winthrip. I'll bet she

24   nearly fainted when she looked in that box.

25 WALLY: *(Warming up)* She was pretty surprised.

26 ANDREW: If she hadn't found you, how long were you going

27   to stay?

28 WALLY: *(Shrugs)* I don't know.

29 ANDREW: If I had hidden in the box, I would have stayed

30   until everyone went home for the night.

31 WALLY: Yeah. Yeah, me, too.

32 ANDREW: It would be cool to be the only one here. I'd like

33   that.

34 PHIL: I wouldn't.

35 WALLY: I would.

1 ANDREW: If I were the only one here, I'd leave messages on
2   all the blackboards. Everyone would go nuts the next day
3   trying to figure out who wrote them.
4 WALLY: I was going to shoot baskets.
5 ANDREW: I didn't know you played basketball. Are you
6   going to go out for the basketball team?
7 WALLY: Naw.
8 ANDREW: You should. You're tall. I'll bet you're good at bas-
9   ketball, aren't you?
10 WALLY: I don't know. I've never played.
11 PHIL: You've never played basketball?
12 WALLY: I have to go now. *(WALLY starts walking again. AN-*
13   *DREW and PHIL walk with him.)*
14 ANDREW: We're thinking of trying out for basketball. Prac-
15   tice starts next week. Why don't you go with us?
16 WALLY: I told you. I don't play basketball.
17 ANDREW: You could learn.
18 PHIL: We aren't very good. You wouldn't be out-classed or
19   anything.
20 ANDREW: That's right. It's just fun to play.
21 WALLY: *(Hesitates slightly, as if tempted to say yes. Then he shakes*
22   *his head no.)* I'm too busy. I've got better things to do than
23   run around some stupid gym. *(He exits.)*
24 PHIL: What a jerk.
25 ANDREW: I feel sorry for him. He's lonely.
26 PHIL: That's because he won't talk to anyone.
27 ANDREW: He talked to us.
28 PHIL: Briefly. Just long enough to tell us he had better things
29   to do.
30 ANDREW: He's afraid.
31 PHIL: Huh?
32 ANDREW: He's scared. He thinks he won't be any good at
33   basketball, so he's afraid to try.
34 PHIL: What makes you think that? Maybe he just doesn't want
35   to play. He said he's too busy.

1   ANDREW: He had time to sit all alone in an empty box. For
2   people like Wally, it's easier not to go out for basketball
3   than to risk getting cut from the team. And it's easier to
4   sit inside an empty box than to try to learn something in
5   class.
6   PHIL: Well, if that's how he feels, there isn't much we can do
7   about it.
8   ANDREW: No. But I wish there were.
9   PHIL: Don't waste too much time worrying about Wally. Now
10   that he got caught, I doubt if he'll go back in that box again.
11 ANDREW: It's Wally's other boxes that concern me. The invis-
12   ible ones. Those are what keep him from learning to play
13   basketball and talking to other kids. They keep him out
14   of class, too.
15 PHIL: Invisible boxes?
16 ANDREW: Invisible boxes that he builds himself.
17 PHIL: Come on. Let's go shoot some baskets. I need the prac-
18   tice.
19 ANDREW: So do I. *(They exit.)*
20
21
22
23
24
25
26
27
28
29
30
31
32
33
34
35

55

FIVE MINUTES
TO CHANGE THE WORLD

1   *CAST:*   Five players, either sex, and CONTROLLER.
2   *AT RISE:*   Characters ONE, TWO, THREE FOUR and FIVE are
3   On Stage.
4
5   ONE: Our parents made a mess of the world.
6   TWO: The oceans are polluted. The air is polluted.
7   THREE: There's overpopulation.
8   FOUR: Oil spills. Litter.
9   ONE: Wars. Famine.
10   THREE: Homelessness. Drugs. Crime.
11   FIVE: Animals are becoming extinct.
12   ONE: Child abuse. Illiteracy.
13   TWO: There are nothing but problems everywhere. The older
14   generation was totally irresponsible.
15   FIVE: If *we* were in charge, this never would have happened.
16   TWO: We would have world peace. And a clean environment.
17   FOUR: If teens ran the world, things would be different.
18   ONE: No one would go hungry.
19   THREE: Give us just five minutes with the world leaders and
20   we could tell them how to improve the whole planet. *(CON-*
21   *TROLLER rushes in.)*
22   CONTROLLER: Stop!
23   OTHERS: Who's that? What? What do you want? *(Etc.)*
24   CONTROLLER: I am Controller. I decide who is in charge of
25   the world. I have heard your complaints, and I think you
26   are right. The world is in a mess. The adults have botched
27   up the job.
28   FIVE: Controller? I never heard about any controller.
29   THREE: Are you God's assistant?
30   CONTROLLER: I am no one's assistant. I am in charge.
31   TWO: Hi, boss.
32   CONTROLLER: I have decided to give you a chance to save
33   the world. Right here. Right now. When I say "go," you will

1	have five minutes to decide what changes you want to
2	make and how you will make them. It is not enough to say
3	you want world peace; you must also say how you plan
4	to achieve it.
5	FOUR: Five minutes isn't very long for such an important job.
6	CONTROLLER: All you must do is tell me how to proceed.
7	I'll see that your plans are carried out.
8	TWO: Do you have anything to do with raising allowances?
9	ONE: Five minutes is better than nothing. Let's do it.
10	CONTROLLER: Ready? *(Others nod yes.)* Go.
11	ONE: I think the first problem we have to solve is hunger.
12	When people don't have enough to eat, they can't think
13	about anything else.
14	FOUR: People in the U.S. should share their food with the
15	poor countries.
16	THREE: We spend millions of dollars a year on diet foods
17	while other people are starving.
18	FOUR: How do we get the food to those who need it?
19	TWO: Let's fly it over and drop bundles down to areas that
20	need food. Can't you just see it? Millions of cupcakes fall-
21	ing from the sky. *(He sings)* "Twinkie, Twinkie, little star."
22	ONE: Who pays for the airplanes?
23	THREE: The government.
24	FIVE: If the government does it, taxes will go up.
25	FOUR: *We* are the government.
26	ONE: We have to be careful that the food doesn't go to un-
27	scrupulous people who sell it on the black market. How
28	do we know who to trust?
29	THREE: What about spoilage? Bread would get stale.
30	FOUR: We would send flour and yeast. Powdered milk. Dried
31	fruit.
32	FIVE: Do those people have ovens? How do they cook?
33	ONE: What about utensils? Bowls and cups? If we send pow-
34	dered milk, do they have something to mix it in? Some
35	way to drink it?

1   TWO: This is getting too complicated. Let's tackle one of the
2   other problems first.
3   THREE: Pollution.
4   FOUR: Yes. Let's get rid of pollution.
5   FIVE: Let's ban all automobiles.
6   TWO: No way. I'm almost through driver's training. I'll get
7   my license in a couple of weeks.
8   THREE: Do you want clean air, or do you want to drive a car?
9   TWO: Both.
10   FIVE: Not just cars. We should ban all motor vehicles.
11   ONE: My dad is a sales rep. Without a car, he'd have no job.
12   TWO: At least we'd know what to do with the extra food. We
13   could give it to you.
14   THREE: Couldn't he call his customers and take orders by
15   telephone?
16   ONE: He has new products twice a year. The store owners
17   want to see them, before they order.
18   FOUR: What about trucks? Should we ban trucks, too?
19   ONE: Without trucks, how would the food get to the super-
20   markets?
21   FOUR: If nobody had a car, we would all shop at neighbor-
22   hood stores.
23   THREE: It would be like the old days. My grandparents are
24   always telling how they grew all their own vegetables, and
25   every year they raised a steer and slaughtered it for meat.
26   ONE: Gross.
27   FOUR: I don't think the manager of the apartment where we
28   live would be too happy if we had a steer on the balcony.
29   TWO: You could have a pig instead. Or chickens.
30   FOUR: There's an old lady in the apartment next to us who
31   gets Meals on Wheels. Without them, she'd never have a
32   decent dinner.
33   FIVE: Maybe we can't ban all motor vehicles.
34   THREE: Who decides which ones are OK and which are not?
35   FOUR: We could allow delivery trucks and business cars, but

1   no personal cars.
2   ONE: There would be a lot of people who suddenly claimed
3   they needed their car for business purposes.
4   FIVE: What about school buses?
5   TWO: Ban the buses! Close the schools. But not until after I
6   finish driver's training.
7   ONE: Think of all the industries that are dependent on people
8   being able to drive. My father wouldn't be the only one
9   out of work. Our whole economy would have to change.
10 CONTROLLER: Your time is half gone.
11 THREE: Half gone! We haven't decided anything yet.
12 FOUR: Air pollution is too complicated. Let's start with some-
13   thing smaller, something we know we can change.
14 FIVE: Overpopulation. How do we get birth control informa-
15   tion to people who need it?
16 THREE: Are there charities that do this? If there are, we could
17   have a fund raiser and give them the money.
18 ONE: Remember the big flap between some parents and the
19   school board last year because birth control information
20   was available at our school?
21 TWO: Right. And I didn't even need it. *(Others all look at him.*
22   *TWO shrugs.)*
23 FIVE: If we do anything to promote birth control, it's sure to
24   cause a controversy.
25 FOUR: Let's start with drugs and alcohol. They cause so many
26   other problems, and none of the parents would object.
27 THREE: Good idea. I say we ban all drugs.
28 ONE: Drugs are already banned.
29 THREE: We could make alcohol illegal.
30 FIVE: They tried that years ago. Prohibition. It didn't work.
31   People kept drinking, only they did it secretly.
32 ONE: Just like they do drugs now.
33 FOUR: It's a problem either way, whether there are laws
34   against it or not.
35 THREE: Then what good does it do to try to change things? It

1   won't make any difference what we decide.

2   CONTROLLER: You have two more minutes.

3   TWO: Maybe our parents weren't totally irresponsible. Maybe
4   they tried to solve some of these problems and weren't
5   able to.

6   FIVE: Our grandparents, too.

7   ONE: Maybe we can't change the whole world. Maybe what
8   we have to do is change ourselves.

9   FIVE: And each of us could try to influence one other person
10   and have them do the same until eventually it makes a
11   difference.

12   THREE: I make a commitment never to use drugs or alcohol.
13   Will you join me?

14   TWO: Not even a beer now and then?

15   THREE: Not even a beer.

16   FOUR: I join you.

17   FIVE: Me, too.

18   ONE: Me, too. And I make a commitment to volunteer at least
19   four hours a month with the Red Cross or the Salvation
20   Army or some other agency that helps feed the hungry
21   people.

22   THREE: I'll go with you.

23   FIVE: I will give up junk food and donate the money I save
24   to a group that helps save endangered animals.

25   TWO: Wow! I've seen you eat. You'll probably save the
26   elephants single-handed.

27   FOUR: I can't stop pollution, but I will pick up litter at the
28   city park. I'll recycle the cans and paper I find and dispose
29   of the other trash.

30   FIVE: That's a great idea. I'll help you do that. I know where
31   we can take recyclable plastic, too.

32   THREE: Five minutes ago, we set out to save the world. Now
33   we're reduced to picking up other people's trash. What's
34   wrong with us?

35   ONE: Nothing's wrong. The problems don't have easy solutions.

1   **FOUR:**   We're being practical. We have to start somewhere.
2   **ONE:**   *(Turns to TWO)* **What about you, *(Name)*? You haven't**
3   **agreed to any of these changes. What do you plan to do?**
4   **TWO:**   **Are there any volunteer jobs where you get to drive?**
5   *(They all stare at him, waiting.)* **All right, all right. When I**
6   **get my license, I won't drive unless it's a necessary trip.**
7   **FIVE:**   **No cruising?**
8   **TWO:**   *(It pains him to say this.)* **No cruising.**
9   **THREE:**   **It's a start.**
10   **TWO:**   **It's a sacrifice.**
11   **CONTROLLER:**   **Time's up. What instructions do you have for**
12   **me?**
13   **THREE:**   **None.**
14   **FOUR:**   **We couldn't figure out any solutions. We had our**
15   **chance to save the world, and we blew it.**
16   **ONE:**   **No, we didn't.** *(Turns to CONTROLLER)* **Here are your**
17   **instructions: Every person is to make one change that will**
18   **benefit the world.**
19   **FIVE:**   **We'll start small,**
20   **ONE:**   **And grow,**
21   **THREE:**   **And become powerful.**
22   **FOUR:**   **Eventually, we'll make a difference.**
23   **ONE:**   **Even if it means personal sacrifice.**
24   **TWO:**   **Like no cruising.**
25   **CONTROLLER:**   **You have used your five minutes well. Your**
26   **instructions will be carried out.** *(CONTROLLER exits, fol-*
27   *lowed by others.)*
28
29
30
31
32
33
34
35

56

ONLY A FEW BEERS

1   *CAST:* Five players: JUDGE, DANIEL, BROTHER, FIANCÉE,
2   FRIEND.
3   *SETTING:* Suggests a courtroom. JUDGE sits behind table or desk.
4   DANIEL sits to one side. BROTHER, FIANCÉE and FRIEND
5   sit together on the other side.
6
7   **JUDGE:**   **Court is now in session. Our first hearing is the case**
8   **of Daniel Modum. Would the accused please stand?**
9   **DANIEL:** *(Stands)* **This hearing is unnecessary. I don't under-**
10   **stand why I have to do this.**
11   **JUDGE:**   **You broke the law.**
12   **DANIEL:**   **All I did was buy a six-pack of beer. That's all. I**
13   **didn't hurt anybody.**
14   **JUDGE:**   **In this state, it is against the law for anyone under**
15   **the age of eighteen to purchase alcohol.**
16   **DANIEL:**   **OK, OK. Why can't I just pay a fine, like I do with**
17   **a parking ticket?**
18   **JUDGE:**   **You'll have an opportunity to pay your fine, but first**
19   **we will proceed with the hearing. Three people have of-**
20   **fered to testify.**
21   **DANIEL:**   **Testify to what? I admitted I bought the beer. Why**
22   **do you need witnesses?** *(He looks around.)* **What did you do,**
23   **subpoena everyone who was in the liquor store that night**
24   **to come and swear I bought a six-pack of beer?**
25   **JUDGE:**   **These people were not present when you bought the**
26   **beer.**
27   **DANIEL:**   **Then how can they testify against me?**
28   **JUDGE:**   **They are not here to testify against you. As you**
29   **pointed out, you have already admitted your guilt. These**
30   **people merely want the chance to tell you about someone**
31   **they loved.**
32   **DANIEL:**   **What kind of a goofy hearing is this?**
33   **JUDGE:**   **You will be seated, please. I call the first witness.**

1   BROTHER: *(Stands)* I am the brother of Natalie Wilcox. The
2   driver of the car that hit her swore he wasn't drunk, that
3   he'd had only a few beers. Natalie was my only sister.
4   She's been gone four years, but my family still has not
5   recovered.
6   Natalie would have graduated from high school this
7   year, if she had lived. When my mother saw the graduation
8   ceremony announced in the newspaper, she burst into
9   tears.
10   JUDGE: Daniel, do you have anything to say to Natalie Wil-
11   cox's brother?
12   DANIEL: No. I'm sorry about his sister, but it doesn't have
13   anything to do with me. I'm not the one who killed her.
14   JUDGE: Next witness, please. *(BROTHER sits. FIANCÉE stands.)*
15   FIANCÉE: I am the fiancée of Adam Morrow. We were high
16   school sweethearts and got engaged during our first year
17   of college. We planned to be married on August thirtieth
18   and then both work part time and go to school part time.
19   We planned eventually to open a business together. And
20   we wanted three kids. We even had their names picked out.
21   Adam was killed four days before our wedding. August
22   twenty-sixth at 7:03 p.m. It was still daylight. The driver
23   of the car that hit him said she had been at a company
24   picnic. She'd had a couple of beers and a glass of wine.
25   That's all, she said. Not enough to impair her judgment.
26   Adam and I will never have children now. *(She starts*
27   *to cry.)* We'll never open that business. I'll never forget him,
28   and I'm here today because I still love him. *(She is overcome*
29   *with sobs and sits down.)*
30   JUDGE: Thank you.
31   DANIEL: How much more of this do I have to listen to?
32   JUDGE: One more. I call the final witness for this hearing,
33   Friend of Ralph Balexy.
34   FRIEND: I used to be like you, Daniel. I thought it was cool
35   to have a few beers and who did it harm? My buddies and I

1 used to meet in the parking lot of the city tennis courts.
2 We sat around and drank and told jokes and talked. Noth-
3 ing bad. And then one night, after one of these outings,
4 the phone rang in the middle of the night. As long as I
5 live, I will never forget that voice. It was the mother of my
6 best buddy, and she was crying so hard, I could hardly
7 understand her. It took a few seconds for it to sink in:
8 "Ralph is dead," she told me. "His car went off the road
9 and ran into a telephone pole." I remember thinking, she's
10 wrong. They've made a mistake, Ralph can't be dead; he
11 brought me home only a couple of hours ago.
12   I was a pall bearer at Ralph's funeral. Have you ever
13 lifted a casket, Daniel? Have you ever watched the body
14 of your best buddy be lowered into the ground? *(DANIEL*
15 *squirms, looks away, doesn't answer.)*
16 JUDGE: You may be seated, Friend of Ralph Balexy. Daniel,
17   is there anything you want to say to these people?
18 DANIEL: No. What can anyone say?
19 JUDGE: The next time you want a six-pack of beer, I hope
20   you will remember Natalie Wilcox, Adam Morrow and
21   Ralph Balexy. You may pay your fine to the Clerk of Court.
22   I thank the rest of you for your testimony. This con-
23   cludes the hearing. *(All exit.)*
24
25
26
27
28
29
30
31
32
33
34
35

57

RED ROSES
FOR A DEAD CAT

1   *CAST:*   Four players: LARRY, ROBYN, FRED, MARIE.

2   *SETTING:*   No special setting required.

3   *AT RISE:*   ROBYN and FRED are On Stage. LARRY hurries in.

4

5   ROBYN: Where's Marie?

6   LARRY: That's why I'm late. Oh, it was awful.

7   FRED: What's wrong? Did something happen to Marie?

8   LARRY: We were just down the street—over by the shopping

9   center—and all of a sudden a cat darted out from between

10   two cars, and Marie couldn't stop in time.

11   ROBYN: Oh, no. Her car hit the cat?

12   LARRY: Killed it. It wasn't Marie's fault. She slammed on the

13   brakes, but there was no way she could have stopped in

14   time.

15   FRED: That's terrible.

16   ROBYN: Poor Marie.

17   LARRY: We heard a thud and knew we'd hit the cat. I told

18   Marie to keep going, that we didn't want to look, but she

19   insisted on stopping. She said it might not be dead, and

20   we would have to take it to a veterinarian. But it was dead,

21   all right. There was blood all over the street, and the cat

22   just lay there. Marie felt it, just to be sure there was no

23   heartbeat.

24   ROBYN: Bleah. How could she stand to touch it?

25   LARRY: I felt sorry for the cat, but I almost felt sorrier for

26   Marie. She was crying and her hands were shaking. You'd

27   have thought she hit some kid instead of just a cat.

28   FRED: Did it have a collar on? An identification tag?

29   LARRY: No. We looked. We were going to call the owners to

30   tell them what had happened, but it didn't have a collar.

31   It was a pretty cat, though, black with white feet, and it

32   looked sleek and well fed. Not like a stray.

33   FRED: It was probably someone's pet, but they didn't get it

1		a tag.
2	LARRY:	That's what we thought.
3	ROBYN:	So where is Marie now? Did she go home?
4	LARRY:	No. She . . . you won't believe this. She went to buy
5		flowers for the cat.
6	ROBYN:	Flowers!
7	FRED:	Are you serious?
8	ROBYN:	What for?
9	LARRY:	She said if it *is* someone's pet, she doesn't want them
10		to go out looking for it and find it dead on the side of the
11		street and think that the person who hit it didn't even care
12		about it.
13	FRED:	The owners didn't care too much about it themselves,
14		or they would have had the cat wear a tag.
15	LARRY:	I told her that.
16	ROBYN:	It might not belong to anybody.
17	LARRY:	She said if it didn't belong to anyone, then the flowers
18		would be for the cat. She said all life is sacred, and she
19		can't leave it there without doing anything.
20	FRED:	Why didn't you get a shovel and bury it?
21	LARRY:	I suggested that, too. Marie said if someone is looking
22		for it and we bury it, then the owners would never know
23		what happened and they'd worry and wonder and go
24		around for days calling, "Kitty, Kitty, Kitty." She said she'll
25		go back in a couple of days, and if the cat is still there,
26		she'll bury it then. Meanwhile, she went to buy some flow-
27		ers, and I walked on over here. *(MARIE enters.)*
28	ROBYN:	Hi, Marie. We're sorry about the cat.
29	FRED:	That was rotten luck, having it jump out in front of
30		your car like that.
31	LARRY:	Did you get some flowers?
32	MARIE:	Yes. Three red roses.
33	FRED:	Roses! Roses cost a buck apiece.
34	LARRY:	Where did you put them?
35	MARIE:	I laid them on top of the cat. If his owner finds him

1   now, he'll know that I am sorry. He'll know that we stopped

2   and made sure the cat didn't need help.

3   FRED: There are hundreds of unwanted cats roaming the

4   streets, you know. Some people would have given them-

5   selves five points for hitting it.

6   ROBYN: That's true. There are mean people who do things

7   like that.

8   MARIE: I know that. That's why I couldn't just drive away

9   and do nothing. Don't you see? It's because there *are*

10   people like that—cruel people who think it's a joke to see

11   an animal suffer—that I had to show my sorrow.

12   ROBYN: The next person down the street could steal the flow-

13   ers. The owner might not ever know that anyone put roses

14   there.

15   FRED: And the cat sure as heck doesn't know.

16   MARIE: But I know. I ended that cat's life—

17   LARRY: Through no fault of your own—

18   MARIE: True, through no fault of my own. But I ended a life,

19   and I had to do something to honor it. Maybe the roses

20   weren't for either the owner or the cat. Maybe the roses

21   were for me.

22   FRED: Man, people driving down the street are going to won-

23   der what the heck's going on when they see a dead cat

24   lying there with three red roses on top of it.

25   ROBYN: They won't know what to say.

26   MARIE: Yes, they will. They'll say, "Someone thought that

27   cat was important."

28   LARRY: And they'll be right.

29

30

31

32

33

34

35

58

SOMEDAY LIFE
WILL BE SWEET

1   *CAST:*   Eight players: RICHARD, SYD, ELLIE, PEG, CARL,
2   BETH, MELISSA, DOUG.
3   *SETTING:*   No special setting.
4   *AT RISE:*   RICHARD, SYD, ELLIE and MELISSA are on one side
5   of the playing area. PEG, CARL, BETH and DOUG are on the
6   other side. All face the audience.
7
8   RICHARD: Man, I can't wait until I finish school. I'll be so
9   glad to quit studying.
10   SYD: When I get my driver's license, things will be great. No
11   more bus. No more begging for rides.
12   ELLIE: As soon as I'm old enough, I'm going to get my own
13   apartment. If I don't, my little brothers will drive me insane.
14   RICHARD, SYD and ELLIE: Life will be sweet when that hap-
15   pens; oh, yes. Someday life will be sweet.
16   RICHARD: Meanwhile, it's the same, old drudgery. Home-
17   work. Tests. Deadlines. It wears me out.
18   SYD: Eventually, I'll have a car of my own. Then I'll really
19   be free.
20   ELLIE: I get so sick of their noise and crying and mess. My
21   house is like living in a daycare.
22   RICHARD: Things will be different when I'm out of school.
23   I'll never open another book.
24   SYD: Things will be different when I can drive. You won't
25   find me on a bus, ever again.
26   ELLIE: Things will be different when I have my own apart-
27   ment. Everything will be quiet and clean. I will never
28   watch another Saturday-morning cartoon.
29   RICHARD, SYD and ELLIE: Life will be sweet when that hap-
30   pens; oh, yes. Someday life will be sweet.
31   PEG: My favorite class this year is speech and drama. I've
32   never memorized so much in my life, but it's worth it.
33   CARL: Six months ago, I started riding my bike to school. My

1   stamina increased so much that I began running a couple
2   of miles every day. I used to feel flabby; now my muscles
3   are firm.
4 BETH: I'm teaching my kid sister to play the guitar. We're
5   going to surprise our grandparents and play a duet for
6   their wedding anniversary.
7 PEG: I'm going to try out for the class play. I hope I get a
8   part, but if I don't, I'll take tickets or usher.
9 CARL: Right now, I'm training to do a triathlon. I don't expect
10   to win it, but I think I can finish. I know I'll never be on the
11   cover of *Sports Illustrated*, but I like to challenge myself.
12 BETH: Even if Susie and I are never great on the guitar, we
13   have a lot of fun practicing.
14 ALL: Life is sweet now; oh, yes; oh, yes. Life is so sweet, right
15   now.
16 MELISSA: My mom has a new boyfriend. They're going to
17   get married next summer. Man, I can hardly wait because
18   he is loaded. I'll be able to buy anything I want.
19 ELLIE: It's rotten to be the oldest child in a family. I always
20   have to be responsible for the younger kids, and I'm ex-
21   pected to do way more work than they are. It isn't fair.
22   When I grow up, I intend to have a maid.
23 SYD: When I have my own car, I'm going to take off and see
24   the world. I can travel cheap. Camp out. Cook over a
25   campfire. Anything to get away from this dull town.
26 MELISSA: Things will be different when Mom gets married.
27   We'll have all the money we want.
28 ELLIE: It will be different someday. Nobody to boss me
29   around, and no bratty, little brothers always whining for
30   me to play with them.
31 RICHARD: Two more years. If I can just make it through two
32   more years, I'll be OK.
33 SYD: Wheels. That's the secret to happiness. Get your own
34   set of wheels.
35 MELISSA: Money. That's the key. When I have enough

1   money, my life will be great.

2   RICHARD, ELLIE, MELISSA and SYD: Life will be sweet

3   when that happens. Oh, yes. Someday life will be sweet.

4   DOUG: I've been doing a lot of babysitting lately. As soon as

5   I save up seventy-five dollars, I can get a cat. The cat is

6   free, but I have to pay for vaccinations and to have it

7   neutered.

8   CARL: Every Saturday, the morning paper prints what's

9   going on around town. Last week, I went to an outdoor

10   jazz festival. Next week, there's going to be a crafts fair.

11   The trouble is, there isn't time to do everything that I'd

12   like to do.

13   DOUG: The kids I sit for are so neat. I'd forgotten how much

14   fun it is to blow bubbles and finger paint and work puzzles.

15   PEG: The first speech I gave was pretty awful. I was so ner-

16   vous my knees shook. But each one got easier and now I

17   look forward to giving my speeches. I feel confident.

18   BETH: I didn't want to move here. I cried and cried when my

19   dad got transferred. But now I wouldn't go back to my

20   old school for anything. I learned there are good people

21   everywhere, and if you're happy within yourself, it doesn't

22   matter where you live.

23   DOUG: I started babysitting for the money. I like it so much,

24   I've decided to be a kindergarten teacher.

25   CARL: There are free travel movies at the library on Wednes-

26   day nights. Each one is about a different state. So far, I

27   liked the one about Arizona best.

28   BETH: My sister used to get on my nerves, but when we

29   moved, I didn't have anyone else to talk to for awhile and

30   I discovered she isn't so bad. Yesterday, she baked coconut

31   cookies, which are my most favorite food in the whole

32   world. She said it was a thank you, for the guitar lessons.

33   PEG, CARL, BETH and DOUG: Life is so sweet right now;

34   oh, yes. Life is so sweet right now.

35   SYD: There is never anything to do in this town. There's no

1   teen center; no place for kids to hang out. Without a car,
2   I am stuck in Dullsville.
3 CARL: I have to miss the next movie, the one on New Mexico.
4   My softball team has a game scheduled that night.
5 RICHARD: Grades, grades, grades. I am sick of worrying
6   about getting good grades. The day I get my last report
7   card will be the happiest day of my life.
8 PEG: I applied for a part-time job last week, and three people
9   interviewed me, all at the same time. Instead of being ter-
10   rified, I was actually relaxed. After all those speeches in
11   class, it was easy to face only three people. I got the job.
12 ELLIE: Privacy. That's all I want. Just a little privacy. And
13   someday, I'm going to have it.
14 BETH: I was so lonely when we first moved. Now I have great
15   friends. We're having a barbecue at my house Friday night.
16   A potluck.
17 MELISSA: I'm going to throw out every stitch in my closet
18   and buy a whole new wardrobe. I can hardly wait.
19 SYD: First my license, then a car, and then I'm out of here.
20 RICHARD, SYD, MELISSA and ELLIE: Someday life will be
21   sweet; oh yes.
22 PEG, CARL, DOUG and BETH: Life is so sweet right now.
23
24
25
26
27
28
29
30
31
32
33
34
35

59

DEAR JAN SLANDER

1   *CAST:*   Eight players, four females, four males: TRISH, JAN SLAN-
2   DER, MOTHER, ELLIE, JEREMY, DARREL, WAYNE,
3   FATHER.
4   *SETTING:*   No setting required.
5   *AT RISE:*   All are On Stage. All except JAN SLANDER have pencil
6   and paper. JAN SLANDER has a whole handful of letters.
7
8   TRISH: Dear Jan Slander: There's this guy I like, named
9   Jeremy, who doesn't notice I'm alive. How do I get him to
10   notice me? Signed: Perplexed.
11   SLANDER: Dear Perplexed: Whenever he looks at you, smile.
12   JEREMY: Dear Jan Slander: There's a girl at my school who
13   is driving me crazy. She follows me around all the time
14   with a simpy grin on her face. How can I get her to stop?
15   Signed: Weary.
16   SLANDER: Dear Weary: Whenever you see her grinning at
17   you, turn away. She'll soon get the hint.
18   JEREMY: Dear Jan Slander: The girl I wrote you about is
19   still grinning. I know she wants me to ask her out, but I'd
20   date my friend's pet rat before I'd go out with her. How
21   do I get her to bug off? Signed: Weary.
22   SLANDER: Dear Weary: You need to be blunt. Come right
23   out and tell her to leave you alone.
24   TRISH: Dear Jan Slander: I think the guy I like likes me, too,
25   because he's always kidding around and telling me things
26   like "Bug off, stupid." How do I get him to ask me out?
27   Signed: Perplexed.
28   SLANDER: Dear Perplexed: Why would you want to go out
29   with someone who calls you stupid and tells you to bug
30   off? I suggest you look for a different boyfriend.
31   TRISH: Dear Jan Slander: Boy, were you ever right. I'm so
32   glad I dumped that Jeremy. His brother, Darrel, is twice
33   as cute and a better football player besides. He hasn't

1   asked me out yet, but I'm still smiling. Signed: Happy Face.

2   DARREL: Dear Jan Slander: Thanks a lot. There's a drippy

3   girl who always used to follow my brother around, until

4   you told her to leave him alone and get a new boyfriend.

5   So who did she choose? You guessed it. Signed: Second

6   Choice.

7   SLANDER: Dear Second Choice: Sorry about that.

8   MOTHER: Dear Jan Slander: I am worried about my daugh-

9   ter. She keeps developing crushes on boys who don't care

10   for her. Today, I had a call from a father who told me that

11   Trish has been making a nuisance of herself, trying to

12   impress this man's sons. Should I tell my daughter about

13   this call? Should I insist she stay away from these boys?

14   Please advise. Signed: Worried Mother.

15   SLANDER: Dear Worried Mother: Tell your daughter about

16   the call at once. When she learns how the objects of her

17   affection feel about her, she'll cool off in a hurry.

18   TRISH: Dear Jan Slander: Whoopee! Darrel must like me even

19   more than I thought because, guess what? His father is

20   jealous! He even called up my mother and told her to keep

21   me away from his son. He's probably afraid we're going

22   to elope. Now that I know for sure how Darrel feels about

23   me, it's easy to keep smiling.

24   DARREL: Dear Jan Slander: You said you were sorry, but I

25   need advice, not apologies. How do I get the grinning girl

26   who likes me to leave me alone? She does not take a hint.

27   Signed: Sick of Her Smile.

28   SLANDER: Dear Sick: Perhaps you could talk frankly to one

29   of her friends and ask them to pass your feelings along.

30   TRISH: Dear Jan Slander: The most romantic thing happened

31   today. During sixth period, Darrel sent a note to my friend,

32   Ellie, and when she opened it, it said, *Dear Ellie, Please*

33   *meet me in the gymnasium after school. I need to talk to*

34   *you about Trish.* Isn't that incredible? The poor, shy fellow

35   wanted Ellie to tell me how much he cares for me. Well,

1   luckily, Ellie showed the note to me and asked me what I
2   wanted her to do. I told her she did not need to act as an
3   intermediary; I would meet Darrel in the gym myself. I
4   did, too. Only when he saw me coming, he was overcome
5   with emotion and ran away. I will treasure the memory
6   forever. Signed: Blissful.
7 DARREL: Dear Jan Slander: Your advice so far stinks. Since
8   I tried to meet with her friend, things are worse than be-
9   fore. Every time I turn around, there she is. I feel like I
10   have an extra shadow. Could you please write to her and
11   tell her to leave me alone? She pays attention to what you
12   say. Signed: Desperate.
13 SLANDER: Dear Desperate: Sorry. If you want someone to
14   leave you alone, you will need to tell her yourself.
15 TRISH: Dear Jan Slander: Ellie just told me that Jeremy told
16   her that Darrel wrote to you about me. Isn't that just the
17   most incredible thing you've ever heard? I mean, here I
18   am, writing to you for advice on how to get him to ask me
19   out, and there he is, writing to you for advice on how to
20   get me to like him. I hope you answer his letter soon.
21   Signed: The Hopeful Happy Face.
22 ELLIE: Dear Jan Slander: I never wrote to a newspaper be-
23   fore, but I think my friend needs help and I don't know
24   what to do. She has a crush on a boy, Darrel, and she
25   follows him around all the time, and whenever he tells her
26   to leave him alone, she just stands there with this cow-eyed
27   smile on her face. The other kids joke about it and call
28   her toothy. I can see that she's making a fool of herself,
29   but I don't know how to make her see that. What do you
30   suggest? Signed: Ellie, Friend of Toothy.
31 JEREMY: Dear Jan Slander: The girl that used to follow me
32   has been following my brother for weeks now. She even
33   waits outside the locker room after football practice. She
34   is making him crazy. What do you think I should do?
35   Signed: Worried Brother.

1 SLANDER: Dear Worried Brother: Don't do anything. Just
2   be glad she quit following you.
3 FATHER: Dear Jan Slander: Is it possible for a fifteen-year-
4   old to sue for sexual harassment, or do you have to be
5   twenty-one? I think my son has a case. Signed: Worried
6   Father.
7 SLANDER: Dear Worried Father: I suggest you see an attorney.
8 TRISH: Dear Jan Slander: You won't believe this, but Darrel's
9   father got so jealous of me that he hired an attorney and
10   the attorney sent a letter to my mother telling her that I
11   had to stop smiling at Darrel. My mother says this is a free
12   country and I can smile at anyone I want to, but I have
13   decided that if Darrel's father is going to interfere with
14   our romance all the time, I would never be happy as Dar-
15   rel's sweetheart, much less his wife. Therefore, I have de-
16   cided to find a new boyfriend. Signed: Trish.
17 WAYNE: Dear Jan Slander: I need help fast. There is this
18   dopey girl at school who has started following me
19   everywhere I go. If I so much as look her direction, she
20   gives me this big, silly grin. How can I get her to leave me
21   alone? Signed: Not Smiling.
22 SLANDER: Dear Not Smiling: Hire an attorney.
23
24
25
26
27
28
29
30
31
32
33
34
35

60

DOMINOES

1 **CAST:** Ten players.
2 **SETTING:** There are ten chairs in a line diagonally across playing
3 area, from Right Front to Left Rear. They are positioned so that
4 the audience sees the profile of anyone who sits.
5 **AT RISE:** Each player stands in front of a chair. PERSON ONE
6 is at Right Front; PERSON TEN is at Left Rear.
7
8 ONE: When I suggested a bake sale to raise money for our
9 club, Ellen said bake sales are boring and not worth the
10 effort. She really cut me down. That's the last time I suggest
11 anything at a club meeting. *(ONE sits down.)*
12 TWO: I'm going to join an exercise club, to help me get in
13 shape. It's expensive, but I think it might be worth it for
14 the trainers and equipment.
15 ONE: *(Turns around to look at TWO)* If you want to exercise,
16 why not do it at home? You don't need to pay someone to
17 show you how to jump rope. *(TWO sits down.)*
18 THREE: There's a help wanted ad in today's paper. It says
19 they need a dishwasher at The Trojan and it says, "No
20 experience necessary." I'm going over there right after
21 school to apply. I've been looking for a part-time job for
22 months, but everywhere I go, they want experience. This
23 ad is the best news I've seen all year.
24 TWO: *(Turns around to look at THREE)* My brother worked at
25 The Trojan for awhile. It was awful. They hire kids for
26 practically nothing and make them do all the dirty work
27 and yell at them all the time. I wouldn't work there if I
28 was starving. *(THREE sits down.)*
29 FOUR: I got my hair styled last night, at a really good salon.
30 Boy, was that great! Usually, I just go to the cheap, quick
31 haircut places, but this was my birthday present from my
32 grandma. I got a shampoo and conditioner, and a style
33 cut and blow dry. I feel terrific!

1   **THREE:** *(Turns around to look at FOUR)* **Who cut your hair?**
2   **Your kid sister?** *(FOUR sits down.)*
3   **FIVE:**   **Well, I made it through my piano recital with only one**
4   **mistake. What a relief. I've been practicing for weeks, but**
5   **I was afraid I'd go completely blank and sit there staring**
6   **at the keys as if I'd never heard of Beethoven in my entire**
7   **life. Instead, it was kind of fun, once I got started.**
8   **FOUR:** *(Turns around to look at FIVE)* **You really blew it in that**
9   **one place. It must make you mad that you could play your**
10   **piece perfectly at home and then, when you get in front**
11   **of an audience, you goof it up.** *(FIVE sits down.)*
12 **SIX:**   **Man, that was a thrill to hit my first home run. When I**
13   **was running around those bases, I felt like I had wings**
14   **and could fly forever. I'll never forget it.**
15 **FIVE:** *(Turns to look at SIX)* **Too bad you hit the home run with**
16   **nobody on base and then struck out when there were two**
17   **runners on. If you had done it the other way around, we**
18   **would have won.** *(SIX sits.)*
19 **SEVEN:** **Wow! I got an A in English. That's a five-credit**
20   **course; it will bring my whole grade-point average up.**
21 **SIX:**   *(Turns to look at SEVEN)* **What happened in algebra? You**
22   **went from a B-minus to a C-plus. You'd better be careful**
23   **or you'll never get into college.** *(SEVEN sits.)*
24 **EIGHT:** **I handled things pretty well last night. I hate it when**
25   **my folks are like that, but I can't change them. Well, I re-**
26   **fuse to let their problem be my problem. I'll never act the**
27   **way they do, so I'm not going to worry about it anymore.**
28 **SEVEN:** *(Turns to look at EIGHT)* **I hear your old man came**
29   **home drunk again last night, and the neighbors had to**
30   **call the cops because he and your mom were fighting.**
31   *(EIGHT sits.)*
32 **NINE:** **James Ellensworth asked me to the prom! I can't be-**
33   **lieve it. I'm actually going to go to the prom. I thought I**
34   **was going to sit at home tomorrow night, trying not to cry**
35   **and pretending it didn't matter, but instead I'll be there**

1   dancing, just like everybody else.

2   **EIGHT:**   *(Turns to look at NINE)* **Talk about a last-minute invi-**

3   **tation. What happened? Did his date get sick?** *(NINE sits.)*

4   **TEN:**   **I saw a terrific movie last night. It was so funny, I prac-**

5   **tically fell out of my chair laughing. It's called "Little Blue**

6   **Riding Hood," and I'm going to go see it again tonight.**

7   *(TEN taps NINE on the shoulder. NINE looks around.)* **Would**

8   **you like to go to a movie with me tonight? I know it's a**

9   **last-minute invitation, but I just decided on the spur of**

10   **the moment to go, and you have such a great sense of**

11   **humor it would be fun to have you go with me.** *(TEN holds*

12   *out a hand.)*

13   **NINE:**   *(Stands and takes TEN's hand.)* **I'd love to. It sounds like**

14   **fun.** *(TEN smiles and faces audience. At the same time, NINE*

15   *reaches other hand toward EIGHT and speaks to him.)* **You**

16   **know something? I really admire the way you refuse to**

17   **let your family problems drag you down.** *(EIGHT takes*

18   *NINE's hand and stands.)* **You're a strong person; I admire**

19   **that.** *(NINE smiles and faces audience.)*

20   **EIGHT:**   *(Holds out hand to SEVEN)* **I hear you got an A in**

21   **English. Congratulations!** *(SEVEN takes EIGHT's hand and*

22   *stands.)* **That's the toughest class in the whole school. Only**

23   **two people got As. You must be really proud.** *(EIGHT smiles*

24   *and faces audience.)*

25   **SEVEN:**   *(Holds out hand to SIX)* **Man, you really belted that**

26   **baseball. I never saw anyone hit a ball so far.** *(SIX takes*

27   *SEVEN's hand and stands.)* **And I never heard such loud**

28   **cheering, either.** *(SEVEN smiles and faces audience.)*

29   **SIX:**   *(Holds out hand to FIVE)* **Your piano piece was terrific.**

30   *(FIVE stands and takes SIX's hand.)* **I don't see how you can**

31   **make your fingers go so fast or remember all those notes.**

32   **It was great.** *(SIX smiles and faces audience.)*

33   **FIVE:**   *(Holds out hand to FOUR)* **Your new haircut is really**

34   **attractive.** *(FOUR takes FIVE's hand and stands.)* **You should**

35   **always wear it that way. You look like someone on a**

1	magazine cover. *(FIVE, smiling, faces audience.)*
2	**FOUR:** *(Holds out hand to THREE)* **I hear you're going to apply**
3	**for a job today. Good luck!** *(THREE stands and takes FOUR's*
4	*hand.)* **No matter how bad a first job is, at least it gives**
5	**you experience and makes it easier to get a better job later.**
6	*(FOUR smiles and faces audience.)*
7	**THREE:** *(Holds out hand to TWO)* **My cousin joined an exercise**
8	**club, and he looks like a new person.** *(TWO takes THREE's*
9	*hand and stands.)* **He says the people there keep him moti-**
10	**vated, and he doesn't get bored like he used to when he**
11	**tried to exercise at home.** *(THREE smiles and faces audience.)*
12	**TWO:** *(Holds out hand to ONE)* **I like your bake sale idea. I think**
13	**we should do it.** *(ONE takes TWO's hand and stands.)* **If Ellen**
14	**doesn't want to participate, that's OK. Let's plan it to-**
15	**gether.** *(TWO and ONE both smile and turn to face audience.)*
16	*(Players at rear move forward, all still holding hands, so that*
17	*all ten are lined up across the front of the stage.)*
18	**ONE and TWO:** *(As they speak, they raise their clasped hands up*
19	*high and keep them there. ONE also raises other hand.)* **Kind**
20	**words bring joy.**
21	**THREE and FOUR:** *(As they speak, TWO, THREE and FOUR*
22	*raise their clasped hands high and keep them there.)* **Kind words**
23	**create happiness.**
24	**FIVE and SIX:** *(FOUR, FIVE and SIX raise clasped hands high*
25	*and keep them there.)* **Kind words offer comfort.**
26	**SEVEN and EIGHT:** *(SIX, SEVEN and EIGHT raise clasped*
27	*hands high and keep them there.)* **Kind words heal.**
28	**NINE and TEN:** *(EIGHT, NINE and TEN raise clasped hands*
29	*high and keep them there. TEN also raises other hand.)* **Kind**
30	**words lift sad hearts and, one by one, fill them with peace.**
31	**ALL:** **Be kind!** *(Together they lower hands and bow.)*
32	
33	
34	
35	

ABOUT THE AUTHOR

Peg Kehret enjoys a dual profession: playwright and novelist. Her funny, heart-warming plays have been produced in all 50 states and Canada, while her books for young people have earned a wide readership and critical acclaim.

Early in her career, Peg wrote radio commercials. Later, she published magazine fiction, articles, light verse, educational scripts and adult nonfiction books.

Among her many honors are the Forest Roberts Playwriting Award, a Children's Choice Award, the Pacific Northwest Writer's Conference Achievement Award, the Young Hoosier Book Award (nominated by Indiana school children), and selection by the American Library Association for its Recommended Books for Reluctant Readers. Her books are frequently on Young Reader's Choice lists for various states and her work has been published in Denmark, Australia, Norway, Portugal, Canada, and Scotland.

Peg and her husband, Carl, live in Washington State. They have two grown children and four grandchildren.

ALSO BY PEG KEHRET

Books for Young People:

Winning Monologs for Young Actors

**Encore! More Winning Monologs
for Young Actors**

Adult Books:

Wedding Vows

ORDER FORM

Meriwether Publishing Ltd.
P.O. Box 7710
Colorado Springs, CO 80933
Telephone: (719) 594-4422 Fax: (719) 594-9916

Please send me the following books:

_____ **Acting Natural #BK-B133** $14.95
by Peg Kehret
Honest-to-life monologs, dialogs and playlets for teens

_____ **Winning Monologs for Young Actors** $14.95
#BK-B127
by Peg Kehret
Honest-to life nonologs for young actors

_____ **Encore! More Winning Monologs for** $14.95
Young Actors #BK-B144
by Peg Kehret
More honest-to-life monologs for young actors

_____ **Spotlight #BK-B176** $12.95
by Stephanie S. Fairbanks
Solo scenes for student actors

_____ **Get in the Act! #BK-B104** $12.95
by Shirley Ullom
Monologs, dialogs and skits for teens

_____ **Theatre Games for Young Performers #BK-B188** $14.95
by Maria C. Novelly
Improvisations and exercises for developing acting skills

_____ **Theatre Games and Beyond #BK-B217** $15.95
by Amiel Schotz
A creative approach for performers

These and other fine Meriwether Publishing books are available at
your local bookstore or direct from the publisher. Use the handy
order form on this page.

Name: _____

Organization name: _____

Address: _____

City: _____ State: _____

Zip: _____ Phone: _____

❑ **Check Enclosed**
❑ **Visa or MasterCard #** _____

                                         Expiration
Signature: _____   *Date:* _____
            (required for Visa/MasterCard orders)

Colorado Residents: Please add 3% sales tax.
Shipping: Include $2.75 for the first book and 50¢ for each additional book ordered.

❑ *Please send me a copy of your complete catalog of books and plays.*

ORDER FORM

Meriwether Publishing Ltd.
P.O. Box 7710
Colorado Springs, CO 80933
Telephone: (719) 594-4422 Fax: (719) 594-9916

Please send me the following books:

_____ **Acting Natural #BK-B133**   **$14.95**
by Peg Kehret
Honest-to-life monologs, dialogs and playlets for teens

_____ **Winning Monologs for Young Actors**   **$14.95**
#BK-B127
by Peg Kehret
Honest-to life nonologs for young actors

_____ **Encore! More Winning Monologs for**   **$14.95**
Young Actors #BK-B144
by Peg Kehret
More honest-to-life monologs for young actors

_____ **Spotlight #BK-B176**   **$12.95**
by Stephanie S. Fairbanks
Solo scenes for student actors

_____ **Get in the Act! #BK-B104**   **$12.95**
by Shirley Ullom
Monologs, dialogs and skits for teens

_____ **Theatre Games for Young Performers #BK-B188**   **$14.95**
by Maria C. Novelly
Improvisations and exercises for developing acting skills

_____ **Theatre Games and Beyond #BK-B217**   **$15.95**
by Amiel Schotz
A creative approach for performers

These and other fine Meriwether Publishing books are available at your local bookstore or direct from the publisher. Use the handy order form on this page.

Name: _____

Organization name: _____

Address: _____

City: _____ State: _____

Zip: _____ Phone: _____
❑ **Check Enclosed**
❑ **Visa or MasterCard #** _____
                                            Expiration
Signature: _____ *Date:* _____
      (required for Visa/MasterCard orders)
Colorado Residents: Please add 3% sales tax.
Shipping: Include $2.75 for the first book and 50¢ for each additional book ordered.

❑ *Please send me a copy of your complete catalog of books and plays.*